Curtains Up!

Theatre Games and Storytelling

BY
Robert Rubinstein

INTERIOR ILLUSTRATIONS BY
Libby Head

fulcrum resources
golden, colorado

Library of Congress Cataloging-in-Publication Data
Rubinstein, Robert E.
  Curtains up! : theatre games and storytelling / by Robert Rubinstein ; illustrated by Libby Head.
     p. cm.
Includes bibliographical references and index.
  ISBN 1-55591-984-7 (alk. paper)
  1. Drama in education. 2. Play. I. Head, Libby, ill. II. Title.
  PN3171 .R77 2000
  371.39'9—dc21
                              00-010015

Printed in the United States of America
0   9   8   7   6   5   4   3   2   1

Book design: Pauline Brown
Cover illustration © 2000 Lisa Van Dusen

www.Fulcrumbooks.com

For all those who performed
so well for so many in the nationally known
Troupe of Tellers from
Roosevelt Middle School (1969–1994)
and for Shoshanna.

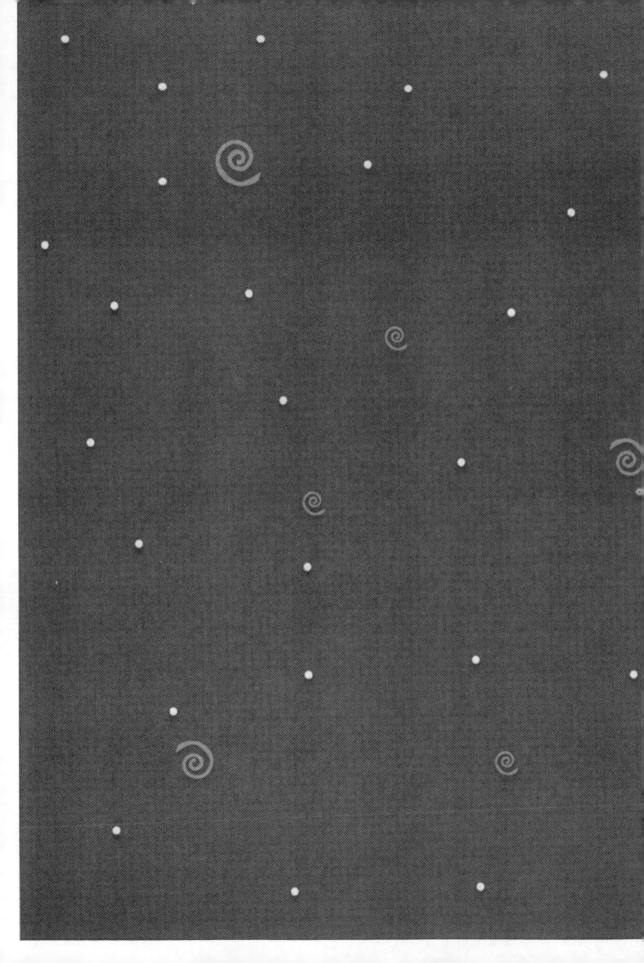

Contents

Curtains Up!

Contents

The Twin Arts of Storytelling and Performing   117

Contents

Acknowledgments

My thanks to Nancy Hopps, Linda Brodie, Richard Leebrick, David Mandelblatt, and Shoshanna Rubinstein for their suggestions and direction, and to all those from whom I've learned about the arts of storytelling and acting. I would especially like to mention Miss Martha Engler, who began my tale at South Boston Public Library, and Judith Sparky Roberts, who teaches in the Lane Community College Theatre Department. Thanks, too, to Gwyn O'Connell, art teacher at South Eugene High School, and to Libby Head, who contributed her artwork to this book. I would also like to acknowledge the technical assistance of Larry Gold and Graham Smith. My appreciation to my editors, Suzanne Barchers and Susan Hill, for their enthusiasm and advice.

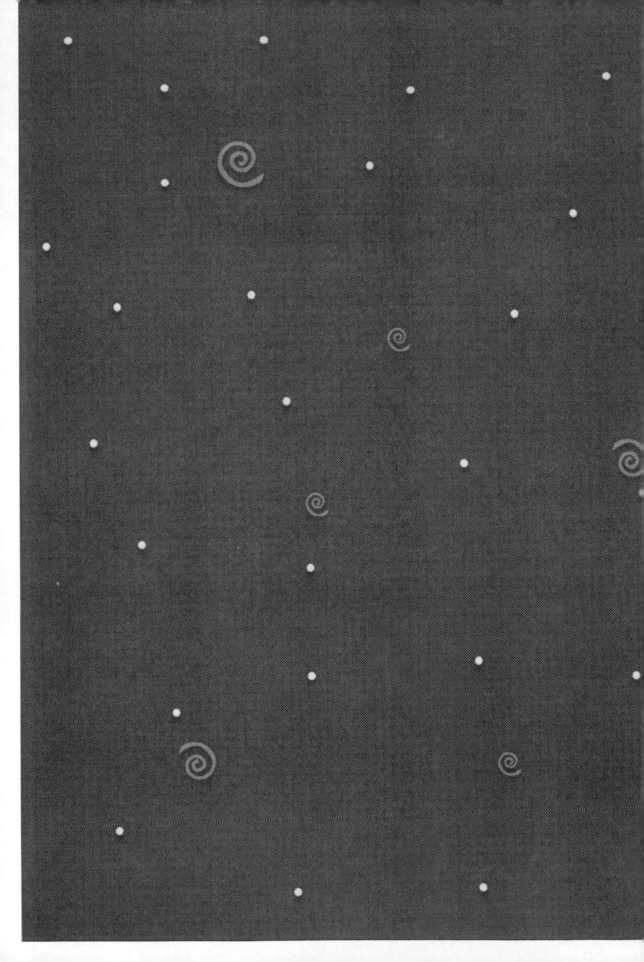

Introduction

Since 1969 I have taught theatre games in my classes at Roosevelt Middle School in Eugene, Oregon. For many years this meant teaching a nine- or twelve-week class titled "Theatre Games" as part of the regular Roosevelt elective curriculum. In this class, students of all abilities and experience had a chance to enjoy, experiment with, and develop their drama, storytelling, improvisation, and speech skills in a safe environment in which they could learn without worry of failing. They enjoy playing The Monster with Three Heads, The Hitchhiker, and Ages of Humankind. Kids should have fun at school—relax in class and look forward to participating as a personal and educational learning experience.

These games and activities learned in the theatre games and storytelling classes helped give many students the confidence and skills to become performing tellers as members of the nationally known Troupe of Tellers from Roosevelt Middle School. Those who did not perform as tellers often used these drama skills in plays, speeches, writing assignments, working with children, or communicating with others in more informal, interesting, and confident ways.

In addition, of course, these activities and the skills learned along with the storytelling experience provide hours of fun with peers, in school and at parties. For twenty summers, members of the Troupe of Tellers staffed the Eugene Public Library's Story Time as volunteers. For this they received one of the state of Oregon's "Great Kids" Community Service Awards.

The Benefits of Laughter

Increasing attention and research are focusing on the benfits of laughter. A wide range of businesses, government agencies, and community organizations have sponsored workshops on how to use laughter to reduce stress and improve the workplace atmosphere.

A Gallup poll shows that 40 percent of Americans feel stressed every day. Thirty-nine percent feel stressed infrequently. Eighty percent of the people who visit doctors with injuries or sickness do so because of stress. Constant or excessive stress can produce rashes, upset stomach, accidents, baldness, breathing and lung difficulties, acne, and high blood pressure, among other health problems. People who feel stressed out cannot think clearly, learn effectively, enjoy life, or make good decisions. They may drink, smoke, take drugs, have violent outbursts of temper, and eat poorly.

Young people can experience all of the above-mentioned problems and concerns even more intensely than adults. Communication problems between young people and adults, or adults' lack of time or patience, may mean that adults often do not listen to young people or understand the stresses placed on them. Young people also have fewer outlets to relieve their stress situations safely and much less access to counseling or guidance than formerly. When these stresses build, they sometimes explode, with tragic circumstances.

Laughter, however, relieves depression, anxiety, stress, muscle tension, and pain. It even provides exercise for muscles and enhances the flow of blood through the body. Humor gives us other ways to view life situations. Laughter can literally be a lifesaver!

So, with these exercises, improvisations, and stories, it's important to maintain that sense of fun. People should enjoy doing these activities, relax with them, laugh—and feel free to create and be innovative. We want others to laugh *with* us, not *at* us—to laugh at what we create and perform for their enjoyment and, possibly, for our own insight. Then their enjoyment becomes our enjoyment and success. All builds from there, and from the self-confidence and good feelings that laughter creates.

For the Teacher or Group Leader

Since humans first came to be, their main means of communication with others has been listening and speaking, not reading, writing, or computers. We tend to forget that in Western culture until a few hundred years ago, most people did not read or write, and yet functioned very well in adult society.

For thousands of years people have shared life experiences and knowledge and learning through acting, performing, and telling stories. These are human moments. These times of sharing became focal points for entertainment, for personal and communal expression, for relieving stress, for passing values and history to the next generation. People tell stories, whether folktales, family tales, or personal experiences, that they want to share so that others may enjoy, understand, listen, and, in some instances, give feedback and direction.

With these activities and storytelling techniques, students gain poise, self-confidence, an outlet for creativity, the opportunity to develop personal communication skills, and an understanding of dramatic techniques and approaches. These are practical skills and knowledge that can be used immediately and that last a lifetime. I've found that through classes in storytelling, students with low skills, those at-risk, and even some with disabilities have experienced success and personal enjoyment. When a student experiences such joy, self-confidence, and accomplishment in sharing, the positive feeling naturally spills over to other academic areas, such as reading and writing.

The teacher can use these games for fun, to help more reticent or at-risk students participate and express themselves, to stimulate thinking and perception, and even for psychological probing and discussion of critical issues.

If students can relax and really enjoy working with a teacher, they will have more trust in that teacher, more willingness to cooperate and learn. As a result, class runs a lot more smoothly.

For Parents

These theatre games and storytelling exercises offer ways for families to come together and have fun; to participate; to share ideas, personal experiences, and perceptions in nonthreatening, nonconfrontational gatherings. Instead of the dullness and passivity of television, these games foster creativity, opening both minds and imaginations. You can take these games and techniques with you anywhere anytime.

The activities are listed so that parents can use an activity that most appropriately matches the age of the child. In most instances, the activities for younger children can be made increasingly sophisticated for use with older children and their particular situations and feelings.

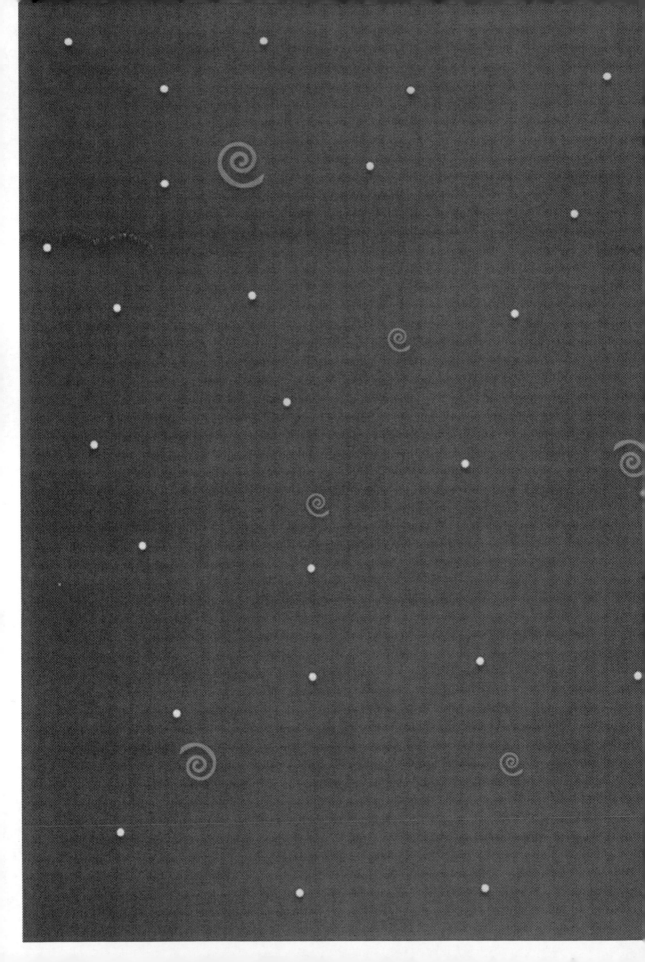

Warm-Ups

Take a few minutes to loosen up and feel freer by doing some warm-ups before you begin the games.

The Cord Through the Body

1. Everybody stands. One person leads the group.
2. Pretend there is a cord running through the center of your body that comes out the top of your head.
3. With this cord through you, feel how it is to keep in balance.
4. Move your body, swaying, back and forth, bouncing up and down on this cord.
5. Think of yourself as a puppet with someone above you pulling on the cord, moving your body, head, arms, and feet.
6. Feel a wind come along and blow you. Then feel the hail coming down upon you.
7. Finally, the sun is warming you. Possibly move to some recorded music.

Stretching

1. Everyone stands.
2. Stand on your toes, then on your heels.
3. Swing your arms side to side, keeping them level. Then swing your arms in arcs.
4. Stretch your arms up overhead.
5. Bend and let your body hang from the waist, arms dangling.

6. Stand and rotate your neck, ear to shoulder, side to side, and then stretching down and back.

7. Rotate your shoulders backward and forward.

8. Move your mouth and jaw side to side and up and down.

9. Scrunch your face and then relax it.

10. With both hands, massage your face and then your scalp.

It's the Face!

Let's focus on the face.

1. Repeat several phrases in a variety of different ways: fearfully, angrily, weakly, strongly, warmly, motherly, authoritatively, mysteriously, evilly, heroically. Each time, stress a different word in the phrase:

> I LIKE you. I like YOU!
> Yeah, like I REALLY like you.

Some phrases follow, but don't forget to make up your own.

Time for dinner!	How are you?
Where is she?	Come over here.
Go to sleep now.	It's cold.
I need some money.	What's the matter?
I don't want to.	We won.

2. While saying these phrases, make appropriate or character facial expressions.

3. Show what you say in your face—with your eyes, nose, mouth, the way you hold your head.

4. You might do this exercise one person at a time, or in chorus as the leader calls out the phrase and the interpretation.

Mirroring

This provides a chance to work on observation and control.

1. In pairs, stand facing each other as if you were seeing your reflection in a mirror.

2. First, one person of the pair makes slow, distinct motions and facial movements, and the partner mirrors these movements as accurately as possible and at the same pace. Remember, the mirror image uses the opposite part of the body. So, if the first person moves the right hand, then the mirror image moves the left.

3. Then let the other person initiate the movements.

Water Walking

This may be done in pantomime first and then later with improvised sounds and exclamations.

1. Everyone stands and walks in a circle.
2. Imagine water flowing into the room, first covering your feet, thighs, and then your waist, neck, and finally over the top of your head—but you discover that you can breathe underwater.
3. Adjust your body movements and gestures according to the changing depth of the water.
4. Then each person becomes a sea creature.
5. After a few moments more, the water recedes slowly. Change your movements in reverse with the lowering of the water.

Some Twists of the Tongue

Not only are tongue twisters fun to say and good for loosening up the group, but they also emphasize concentration and articulation. Good practice! Try repeating these several times in a row:

- Many marbles made Marvin merry.
- Three gray geese in the green growing grass.
- The sixth sheik's sixth sheep's sick.
- Lavinia Lyman lost leaking lemon liniment.
- I never felt felt feel flat like that felt felt flat.
- An old scold sold a cold coal shovel.
- Percy Pig is plump and pink! I like a plump pink pig— I think.
- White Whitney whistled while he whitewashed the fence.
- Six long, slim, slick, slimy, slender saplings swaying in the spring sunshine.
- How much wood would a woodchuck chuck, if a woodchuck could chuck wood? A woodchuck would chuck all the wood he could if a woodchuck could chuck wood.

Walk Through Time

1. Have the group form a circle and begin walking.
2. As they walk, call out characters: toddler, drunk, elderly, person, cowboy, soldier, weakling, strongman, movie star, pregnant woman, and so on.
3. Each person then assumes a walk and a manner that would be typical of that character.
4. As a variation, call out the "character walks" in reverse.

Think Quickly!

This is an exercise that emphasizes listening to others and making responses that require quick thinking.

1. Invite five volunteers to form a line or a semicircle.
2. Whomever you point to must begin talking, without pause, on any topic.
3. When you point to a different person, that person must immediately pick up the topic of the first speaker and continue on, changing the topic when he or she can.
4. Then point to the third person, and so on.
5. If one of the five becomes confused, pauses more than five seconds, or doesn't continue the topic, then that person must sit down.

6. This process continues until one person remains.

7. From the winners of each group, have a play-off to decide the champion.

Do Something Musical

1. Find out who has talent singing, playing an instrument, or dancing. If some don't feel they have these talents, they can improvise or pantomime as if they did: sing, create strange dances, or play real or made-up instruments (wooden spoons, glasses of water, etc.)

2. Now organize the performers into some type of setting (a circus, spaceship, haunted house) or theme (entertainment, family, war and peace, laughter), and have them rehearse for a short time.

3. Stage the musical extravaganza. This is not an award-winning talent show. This is musical expression bordering on chaos!

4. Consider having a more general show with mimes, people doing impersonations or accents, comedy routines, juggling, and so on.

Music Images

1. Play an audiocassette of different instrumental pieces, rhythms, beats, and moods.

2. Have the group close their eyes and see the scene created by the music.

3. In pairs, the group shares with each other what they experienced and "saw" listening to the music. After this, they might volunteer to share their visions with the group.

4. Each pair might merge their visions into an improvised dance piece or series of movements.

Create a World

1. Pretend that it's the beginning of the world.

2. Ask for imaginative suggestions about how the world began.

3. As the person describes the world's creation, have one or two others come up and become that part of the creation.

4. Ask for more suggestions.

5. As each succeeding item or stage of creation is suggested, have others come up to perform. (For example, air, water, the earth, clouds, wind, birds, mammals, insects, sea creatures, humans, houses, fire.)

6. Finally, the entire group is participating in this newly created world.

7. Afterward, a different speaker may begin creating another world.

Folklore Version

Research or read some creation tales from different peoples and incorporate them into the scene. Virginia Hamilton's *In the Beginning: Creation Stories from Around the World* (Orlando, Fla.: Harcourt Brace Jovanovich, 1988) is an excellent resource.

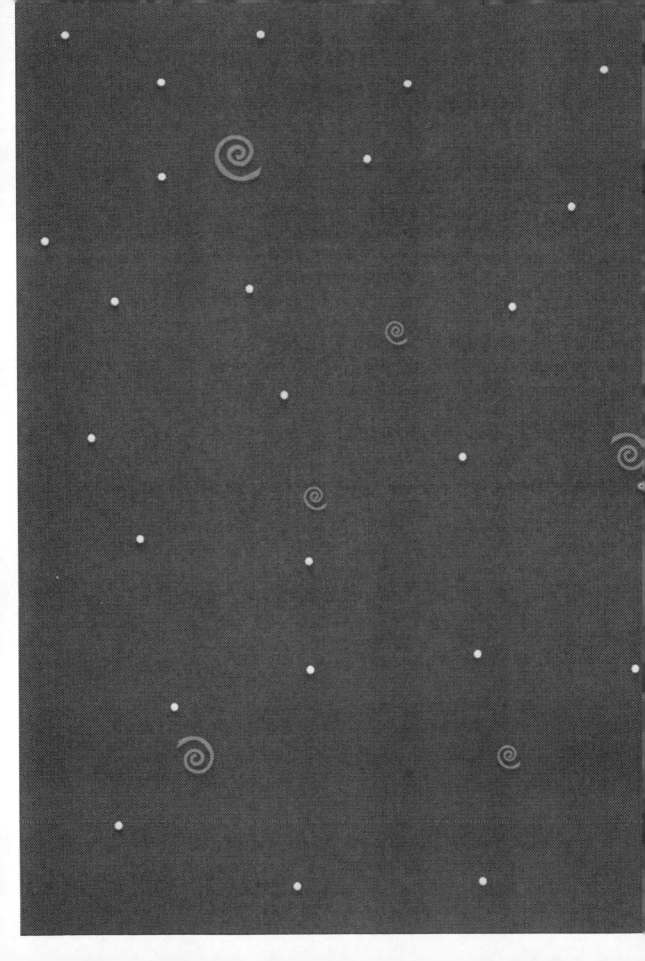

The
Activities

Chain Stories

1. Have the group sit in a circle or in concentric circles.
2. One person says a word, then the next person adds a word, until there's a complete sentence. Continue until some type of story emerges.
3. Perhaps stop for a moment to ask what has happened so far, or what some think may happen next. Then continue adding words and sentences together.
4. The next step could be the one-sentence chain story. Each person adds a sentence to whatever came before in the circle.

Advanced Version

The chain story becomes a timed tale. Each person in the circle speaks for one or two minutes. Even if someone pauses or doesn't know what to say next, everyone waits until that person's time is up. (It's amazing just how long one minute can seem!)

If you happen to be seated in concentric circles, the inner circle of people might tell the tale. After the story is done, the outer circle of people might summarize what they heard as well as what hindered the story from being better and how the telling might improve. (Often, those who are telling begin to repeat the same incidents over and over; actions are just strung together with little embellishment; there's little character, background, or scene detail; and very little dialogue has been included.)

Now that the group knows some ways to improve a story-telling, start another chain story focusing on these ingredients. The outer group becomes the inner one and does the telling this time.

Afterward, evaluate the story again. See how the telling has improved and what still could be developed. After all, a story—especially an oral one—is always in the process of developing, evolving, in need of revision—a good thing for young people to understand and learn.

How Do You Train Your Pet?

P et owners are responsible for training and caring for their pets. Have the group choose a pet—the more un-usual, the more challenging. Ask the owner(s) to think of specific actions or activities they want their pet to do or not do: eat or not eat certain things, fetch, sleep, guard, play, special tricks.

Here are some pets to consider:

Elephant	Penguin
Eel	Hippo
Dinosaur	Mosquito
Eagle	Goose
Termite	Panther
Crocodile	Opossum

Statues

T his is a good exercise for creativity, group organization, and agreement.

1. Form into groups of three to five people.
2. Each person is responsible for creating a statue. The group, in turn, forms a group statue composed of all members (statues) of that group in some type of formation.
3. The group assigns a number to each statue, from 1 to however many statues the group has created. The group rehearses changing from one statue to another as quickly as possible when that statue's number is called.
4. The groups stand, each in their own area. When you call out "Number 1!" each group forms into statue number 1. When you call out "Number 2!" the groups form their statues numbered 2—and so on.
5. Once you have called out all the statues in order and the groups have simultaneously formed their statues, it's fun to call the numbers out of order: perhaps number 5, then number 2, then number 4. The groups must then change to whatever number statue is called.
6. Each group might perform its set of statues for the class.

Body Alphabet

1. Form into groups of three to five people.

2. Each group creates its own body alphabet, using a position of the body to form each letter.

3. Once the group has created the alphabet body positions from A to Z, then each member should rehearse those positions. A member of the group might call out a letter and each person in the group takes the body position representing that letter.

4. Now, have a spelling contest. Write a five- to seven-letter word on paper and show it to one member of each group. That person returns to the group but does not reveal the word. Upon your signal, he or she spells out the word, using that group's body alphabet. The first group to guess the word wins.

5. Try another word with a second person from each group performing, and so on.

Those -*ly* Ending Words

1. Choose three people: two to be actors and one to be recorder-director.

2. The two actors leave the room.

3. The recorder-director then asks the rest of the group for suggestions of -*ly* ending words: lovingly, hatefully, spitefully, proudly, ferociously, vacantly, nosily, bossily, cowardly, and so on.

4. The recorder-director writes down seven of the suggested words.

5. The two actors return to the room.

6. The recorder-director then chooses any of the words at random and calls out the -*ly* ending word. The actors must immediately improvise a situation based on that word as the main emotion.

7. The recorder-director calls out "Freeze!" and gives the next word. The actors switch into a different situation that demonstrates the second -*ly* ending word.

Can You Explain This?

sk the group to be creative in explaining why and how these things actually happened:

- At one time, the Netherlands was known as the United States.
- Spiders, flies, and termites have more protein pound for pound than does beef.
- The only two places in the world where men manage to outlive women are southern Asia and Iran.
- If you live in Cleveland, you cannot catch mice without a hunting license.
- On one occasion, the yellow pages listed a funeral parlor under "Frozen Foods."
- Of all the nations in the world, Icelanders drink the most Coca-Cola.
- In their first year of life, puppies grow ten times faster than human babies.
- If you get married at Disney World, you can have Goofy or Mickey as a guest at your wedding.
- In Oklahoma, it's illegal to get a fish drunk.

 The Robots

Choose two or three people to act out a scene. They must speak and move as robots would. Consider adding one crazy inventor to the group and having them act out a scene.

The Monster with Three Heads

1. Choose three people to come to the front of the group: one of one gender, and two of the other. Also select a moderator.

2. The single girl or boy should stand between the other two. They should be close together, perhaps with arms about each other's waists, because they are one monster, equal to one body with three heads.

3. Each head can speak only one word at a time in rotation with the other two heads.

4. Each statement made by the monster must be a complete sentence. It should not be a yes/no type of answer.

5. The moderator asks questions and/or solicits questions from the audience to ask the monster about its life, behavior, and thoughts. The questions should require an

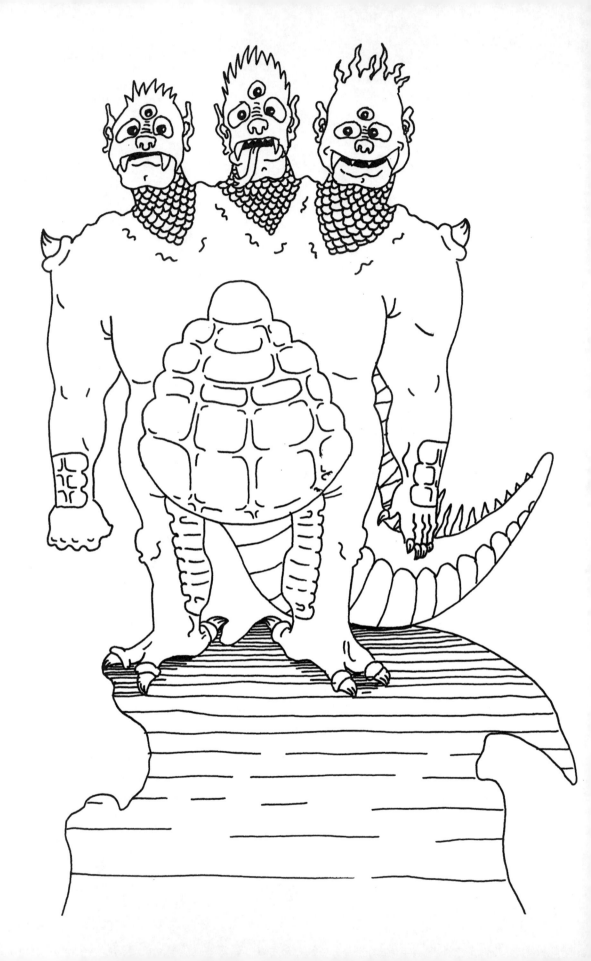

answer that is an explanation or a description, not a one- or two-word reply. If the question needs to be rephrased, then the moderator should ask the person to do so. If the monster does not answer or avoids answering the question, the moderator directs the monster to answer the question. If the monster's answer is not a complete sentence or sentences, or one head says more than one word in turn, then the moderator has the monster correct itself.

6. The moderator may also probe more deeply by asking questions related to the one already asked.

7. Each monster's round or time might be five minutes or five questions. Then choose three more people and a different moderator.

To Start

The moderator announces, "Right here with us today, folks, we have a monster with three heads! Each head can speak only one word at a time. At our request, the monster has been gracious enough to permit members of the audience to ask it questions—and it will answer each question as best it can. Who would like to be the first to ask a question of the monster with three heads?" (If no one raises a hand, then the moderator may start by asking the monster a question. Questions might be: How do you dress? What do you like to eat? How do you go out on a date? What do they call you, and why did they select that name for you?)

Advanced Version

If you choose to do this activity later when people are more at ease and sophisticated in theatre games, you can—especially with a class or church group—question the monster at a deeper level.

- What names do people call you?
- How do you feel when people call you these names?
- How do people react to you? How do you feel about this?
- Now that you have normal parents and siblings What is your family life like?
- How do your parents treat you and feel about you?
- Do your siblings make fun of you? How does this make you feel?
- Do you feel others are prejudiced against you because of your appearance? In what ways are they prejudiced?
- Why do you think people act this way toward you?
- What activities or life experiences have you missed out on or not participated in because of your appearance? How does this make you feel?
- If you could change anything about yourself, what would you change and why?
- What are your hopes and dreams for the future?

After these questions and responses, the group might discuss the monster's replies, feelings, and reactions, and what the statements reveal about the monster and prejudice, as well as about so-called normal people. How do these responses and feelings relate to people from different racial groups, members of minorities, and people with special needs in our society?

Comic Strip

1. Have each person in the group bring in one or two favorite comic strips from the newspaper.
2. Taking turns, each person who brought in the strip chooses others to act out the characters and situation in the comic.
3. They rehearse and perform for the class using character voices, approximate dialogue, gestures, and movements.
4. If the comic strip situation needs a beginning and a conclusion for better audience understanding, the group should improvise these.

Another approach is to have everyone put all the comic strips into a pile, and each person draws one out at random. Then a comic strip is acted out. Or, after acting out the comic strip situation with dialogue, act it out immediately once or twice in pantomime only.

Can't Say No!

Sometimes a person doesn't want or like to do something. In this activity, one person asks another to do an action or task, and a refusal is required. But the person asked cannot simply refuse to do the action or task. Not coming to an agreement, or doing nothing, is unacceptable. Instead, the person asked must persuade the other person to agree on something more acceptable, or to offer another idea for an activity. (The activity could be to put on a hat, laugh, tell a joke, walk backward, or pretend you hurt your arm.)

The person asked might use terms such as:

> Let's try ...
> Why not do ...
> What about this ...
> What would happen if ...
> Would you be willing to ...
> Could we ...

To focus on a serious issue, one person could make a proposal for dealing with crime, the environment, global warming, gangs, smoking, money cutbacks, education, or whatever. If the other person does not like the idea, he or she must propose another one.

Act Out That Song

1. Have the leader or each member of the class write out or copy song lyrics that tell a story. They may be ballads, folk songs, popular songs, nursery songs, or children's songs.
2. Then form into small groups of three to five. Each group selects a song from the pile of song lyrics. Then the group organizes and acts out that song for the class.

The group may tell the title of the song beforehand. One member of the group reads the lyrics of the song out loud before the group acts the song out. Or the group might withhold the song title, act out the song, and have the class guess the title.

Doing the Pants

The following are examples of pantomime scenes to be done individually or in pairs:

- You are a finalist in the National Bubble Gum Blowing Contest. After repeated tries, you blow the biggest bubble ever seen.
- You are a lion tamer. You enter the cage ready to perform your routine when you suddenly remember that the lions have not been fed!
- You are chasing butterflies in the woods. It's exciting until you realize you're lost and will have to spend the night in the woods.
- You're out camping. Set up camp, unload your pack, pitch a tent, chop and collect wood, rub two sticks together for a fire, fry two eggs and some bacon, eat.
- You are from France and speak very little English. You get off the boat in New York City. You ask several people where a restaurant and a hotel are. People can't understand you very well.
- You are a cop in a patrol car. You see a car speeding. You chase and stop it, giving the driver a ticket.
- You are a famous actor or actress auditioning for a dog food commercial—and you hate dogs. The first dog is a dachshund, the second dog is a Saint Bernard.

- You are taken to the principal's office for fighting. At first you're angry and mouth off at the teacher. As you get to the office, you become worried. Then the principal gets you!
- You are in a haunted house. Things keep popping out at you. You are alone and very scared.
- You brag about how well you can play the violin, even though you have never played one. Then someone gives you a violin and insists that you play.
- You are a kangaroo chasing a bird and you bump into an apple tree. Apples tumble down from the tree and hit you in the head. You recover and hop away.
- You are a new window washer. You are washing outside windows twenty floors high. A strong wind starts blowing.

These scenes can be performed by the very shy and reluctant person, or by the person who can act with fine expression and detail. As long as a person performs a pant in front of the group, even for just fifteen seconds, he or she should receive encouragement and recognition.

⊚ Sell
⊚ Your Partner ⊚

1. Have the group divide into pairs.

2. Each member of the pair interviews the other, asking about age, special interests, dislikes, place of birth and where he or she has lived, favorite and worse subjects, pets, hopes or fears, and so on.

3. Have the groups sit down. Call one pair up to the front of the room. One of the two introduces his/her partner and then proceeds to tell the group why the partner would be an exceptional person to have as a friend, servant, or astronaut, doctor, jungle guide, or whatever, now or in the future. Allow three to five minutes per person.

4. The person selling the partner may include some creative humorous stories or other anecdotes about the partner; that's fine. However, these anecdotes must be positive and help sell the partner.

5. Then either have the other partner start selling, or have the pair sit down and call up another pair from the group.

Leaving Planet Earth

It's your last day on Planet Earth. What would you do during this day? Whom would you want to be with? Why would you choose to do these things and be with this person or people?

The Animal Assembly Line

Here's an activity that allows everyone to use whatever drawing skills they have.

1. Using a factory assembly line as a model, have the group "assemble" a cartoon animal character.

2. Divide the group into thirds. Give each person a blank sheet of paper and have them fold the paper into thirds as if they were folding a legal-sized letter.

3. Each person in the first group draws only a head on the top third of the paper each person has. (This could include face, ears, hair, a hat, antlers, etc.) Each person in the second group draws only a body on the middle third of the paper. (This could include neck, belly button, hair, clothes, skin, scales, etc.) Each person in the third group draws only legs and arms on the bottom third of the paper. (This could include feet, toes, hands, fingers, nails, hair, scales, gloves, hooves, shoes, claws, etc.)

4. The first group draws heads on the top third of the paper, leaving the body and leg-spaces empty. Simultaneously, the second group draws bodies in the middle portion of the paper, and the third group draws legs and arms in the bottom space.

5. After five minutes or so, have each group pass the papers to the next group on the assembly line. Now the first group draws heads in the empty top third of the paper. The second group draws bodies under the heads the first group drew. The third group draws legs and arms on the second group's bodies.

6. After another five minutes, have the papers exchanged again, and each group will draw in the missing body section.

7. When the animal characters have been assembled, each person now holding the completed drawing must explain that creation to the class. This might include describing the physical characteristics of the animal, where it was born and how it lives, food it likes and dislikes, any special powers it has, and how it cares for its young.

Another approach is to have each person holding the completed drawing write a caption or a bit of dialogue for the drawing.

The Director

1. Ask for six volunteers. Select one to be the director; the other five are speakers.

2. Assign each speaker a topic. For example, speaker 1 might talk only about hats, speaker 2 about onions, speaker 3 about hockey pucks, speaker 4 about tuba players, and speaker 5 about anteaters. It's a good idea to vary subject areas so that no two people have a topic in the same subject area.

3. Each person speaks in turn on his or her topic for one minute. The first round could be a general description and uses for that topic. Be imaginative and improvise. For the second round, each speaker could talk about a real or imagined personal experience with that topic. The third round could be one of the following: a funeral oration, a salesperson selling that topic, a tabloid, an evening newscast, or a sports event.

4. The director stands behind the speakers. To start, the director taps one person on the shoulder. When thirty seconds are up (if there are long periods of silence, add some time), the director taps that person to stop speaking and then taps one of the other four to continue, proceeding until each speaker has had a turn in that round.

5. When the next speaker begins, he or she must repeat the last sentence spoken by the previous person and weave it into his or her topic.

6. Then the director taps the second speaker to stop, and moves on to the third—until one round is done.

7. When the first round is finished, do the second round.

The director is responsible for keeping track of time; starting, stopping, and changing speakers; making certain that each person speaks only on the assigned topic, and that the next speaker repeats the last sentence of the previous speaker.

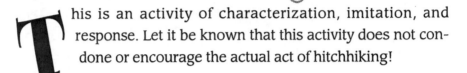

The Hitchhiker

This is an activity of characterization, imitation, and response. Let it be known that this activity does not condone or encourage the actual act of hitchhiking!

1. Select three people: a driver, a front-seat passenger, and a hitchhiker.
2. Set up three chairs in the front of the room: two chairs form the front seat of the car and one chair behind them is the backseat.
3. The driver and front-seat passenger are traveling along, chatting with each other (not about the weather or where they're going!), when they see a hitchhiker on the side of the road. They stop to pick up the hitchhiker.
4. The hitchhiker sits down in the backseat and assumes a character type, such as a witch, lawyer, nerd, three-year-old, one who speaks only in numbers, a detective, a lunatic, an absentminded professor, elderly woman, astronaut, alien, a superhero, or a mom. The hitchhiker must speak on topics and in language suitable for the character portrayed.
5. The driver and front-seat passenger must then imitate whatever character the hitchhiker is, using the same language, pacing, and speaking topic. They may either agree or disagree with whatever the hitchhiker says.
6. After three to five minutes, the driver must find a logical way to stop the car and have the hitchhiker exit.

Vacation Slides

1. Choose three to five actors and one narrator.
2. The narrator stands off to the side so that he or she can see the actors. The narrator says "Click" and begins, "I once went on a vacation to ..."
3. The actors form a spontaneous scene and freeze.
4. The narrator must then describe what is happening in this vacation slide. The narrator does not know in advance what type of scene the actors will form.
5. When the description of the first slide is finished, the narrator says "Click" and continues, "I then went on ..." or "Next, we ..."
6. The actors have formed a second vacation slide. The group could continue for three to five slides.

Let's Argue

1. Select two people. The pair chooses a role to play: any person, any age, in any situation, in any location. Examples are:
   - a mother and daughter
   - Romeo and Juliet
   - Julius Caesar
   - baseball players
   - a rock musician and a fan
   - the president of the United States and his daughter

2. One person of the pair begins an argument. The other responds. (Do not allow yes/no, or "I am/you're not," or "I'm right/No, you're not" arguments.) The argument must escalate and expand with detail, emotion, evidence, and a conclusion.
3. After two minutes of the argument, have a third person come up to side with one of the two arguers.
4. After another minute or two, the person with the minority opinion finds a logical way to exit. Stop the scene.
5. The two people left on stage begin a different argument as different characters in a different time and place.
6. When the third person joins in, that person sides against the one who has been on stage the longest.
7. Afterward, those on stage might discuss how each felt during the argument. What happened when it was two against one? How might the argument have been improved as a conflict or scene?

Ages of Humankind

1. Choose four pairs of people from the group to come to the front of the room.
2. As in "The Director" activity, choose a variety of topics, one per pair, to be discussed. It might be that the first pair can talk only about groundhogs, the second pair about hamburgers, the third pair about teenagers, the fourth

pair about toothbrushes. Each pair must talk about their subject in each round as would one of the following:

- three-year-olds (note that the language pattern and word choice should be for that age)
- teens about fifteen or sixteen years old
- parents with children
- elderly people, with one of the two about to die

3. Then choose some other pairs of people and different topics to try this activity again.

Human Puppets

1. Choose two or three people to act out a scene as human puppets.

2. They should move and talk as if they had strings attached and were being manipulated by a puppeteer.

3. Another person might play the puppeteer and speak his or her own inner thoughts as dialogue.

The Key

1. Choose a person to come to the front of the room.
2. Give this person a real or imaginary key, and say that there's a locked door before him or her.
3. The person puts the key in the lock, opens the door, and describes what is there.

Advanced Version

The person describes why the room is there and what it means to him or her.

The Newspaper in Action

The daily newspaper contains a wide range of possible dramatic situations. Choose a news story, then a narrator, and have people act out the story by playing the roles and improvising dialogue.

Advanced Version

For more challenging newspaper situations, create a drama based on one of the ads in the personal column, or combine three or four advertisements and see what happens.

The Best Marriage Proposal

1. Choose a person to come to the front. Then choose three people of the opposite sex.
2. Each of the three makes the most heartfelt, businesslike, or rational marriage proposal he or she can to the first person.
3. The person receiving the proposal can ask questions of the person proposing.
4. The person receiving the proposal then chooses who will be his or her wedded mate.

The What-Ifs

Another story-starter approach is to simply take some time to let minds wander—even off to the Land of the Absurd of the What-ifs. So:

- What if you suddenly discovered you had an identical twin?
- What if you could fly by simply pressing on your nose?
- What if you could attach body parts to make a strange living creature?
- What if you found out your mother was an alien?

- What if you were a rock and could think, feel, and move?
- What if you could choose to go on the most exciting adventure possible?

You Came from Another Planet

You're an alien whose mission is to visit Earth from a distant planet and then to return with your evaluation of Earthlings. It's now time to report on what you observed and to evaluate human behavior. Discuss, in the English you learned, some of the following from your alien point of view, using examples of what you experienced:

- How humans treat each other
- What entertainment they like
- Fears they have
- What humans value
- Humans' appearance and dress
- Types of transportation
- Use of language and sound
- Music

The Monster Meal

I t's dinnertime and the monsters are hungry! They will gather around the table for good "dinner conversation." Who would you invite to this dinner? What would the conversation be like? What's on the menu—and what's not?

Remember to keep in the character. The character conversation will develop better and more easily if you focus on actual things that happened. You might discuss historical events, movies, food, entertainment, school, families, finding jobs. Describe with detail, feeling, and dialogue as if each character were telling a story.

Here are some possible characters:

- Frankenstein
- Medusa
- Martian
- Dracula
- The Wolf Man
- The Invisible Woman
- Man of a Thousand Faces
- The Phantom of the Opera
- King Kong

The Human Storyboard

1. Choose a folktale and make a list of what happens in the order the events occur in the story.

2. Assign each event in the story to a different person.

3. Have the group line up in the order of the events.

4. Begin telling the story by having each person in turn act out what happens during his or her assigned part of the tale.

5. You might try switching people into a different order and see how the story turns out then.

Advanced Version

Do a human storyboard about the events in a movie, a novel, or a play.

Scene Call-Outs

A scene call-out is the direction a director gives when he or she calls for two characters to play a scene. Have the entire group do a scene, or divide into smaller groups, each of which will do the same scene with its own interpretation simultaneously. You might first do these scenes as pantomimes, and then later repeat them with improvised dialogue.

Here are some examples to try—and then you might invent your own:

- an orchestra
- welcoming aliens
  to Earth
- a haunted house
- a town on the moon

- a funeral
- kindergarten
- a wedding
- a hospital

Interview an Expert

1. Select one person to be the expert and send him or her out of the room.
2. Select another person to be the interviewer.
3. The group decides what type of expert the person will be when he or she comes back into the room. Here are some possibilities:
   - anteater trainer
   - flügelhorn soloist
   - specialist in
     caveman cooking
   - Chinese archaeologist
   - toilet bowl cleaner
4. The group also makes up a name for the expert, but this name should not give away the expert's area of expertise.

5. The interviewer invites the expert into the room, to be seated, and introduces the expert by name. The interviewer asks the expert questions about his or her expertise without revealing what the person does. For example, if the expert trains anteaters, the interviewer might ask, "If you like animals, what type? I heard you are partial to very extended noses. Why is that? If you have termite problems in your house, what have you done to solve them?" The questions should not require yes or no answers but ask for more detail and explanations. The situation becomes funnier as the details and answers become more inappropriate with regard to the area of expertise.

6. The expert must guess what his or her expertise is.

"No News" Day

It's a "no news" day at the daily paper. Nothing major seems to be happening. Here is an opportunity to create news out of some very plain objects:

- rye bread
- a notebook
- false teeth
- a pillow
- cotton candy
- a mouse hole
- a thermometer
- a baseball cap

- a puppy
- fig leaves
- a telephone book
- a tire
- Bugs Bunny
- dental floss
- a globe
- a stuffed aardvark

A Panel of Experts!

A panel of experts discusses vital problems we face today. This panel may consist of any four or five of the following: a psychiatrist, social worker, economist, teacher, parent, teen, cook, pilot, mechanic, minister, cartoonist (you may choose others). Each panelist speaks as an expert in his or her field, and in language one would expect to hear from such an expert. Panelists may decide to discuss topics either seriously or humorously.

- running away
- sportsperson's salaries
- future jobs
- space travel
- natural resources
- world peace
- driving illegally
- heroes and heroines
- junk food
- schools
- insects

The Expert and the Demonstration

1. Choose three people:
   - One person is a foreign expert who does not speak any English.
   - The second person demonstrates what the expert is describing.
   - The third person is the interpreter, who creatively explains what the expert is saying and the demonstrator is doing.

2. The interpreter introduces the foreign expert as a doctor or professor or some other title. The interpreter also decides what that expert's area of expertise will be— for example, garbage, snakes, tires, beehives, bike bells, toys, or lightbulbs.

3. The audience may also ask questions, which, of course, the interpreter must translate into whatever language the expert speaks.

Explain, Please

Take a moment to think about the following statements. How would you explain them?

- When cheese has its picture taken, what does it say?
- When we say something is "out of whack," what exactly is a whack?
- We define "horrific" as meaning horrible. Why doesn't "terrific" mean terrible?
- Why do "wise man" and "wise guy" mean the opposite?
- If "a fool and his money are soon parted," where does the fool go and where does the money go?
- What does a tux tuck?
- Concerning the quotation "The best-laid plans of mice and men," what plans do mice make?
- How do you find a needle in a haystack?
- Concerning the statement "If I only had a brain!" what would you do?
- "Life is just a bowl of cherries." How do you live life in a bowl of cherries?
- How do you know "a dog is man's best friend"?
- Why are people from Poland called "Poles"? Why aren't people from Holland called "Holes"?

Look at Familiar Situations

This activity is about life situations that happen to nearly everyone at some time. Reenact each of these situations—either as each might be, or with some humorous or more tragic twist. Focus on creating dialogue and character rather than a string of actions and violence.

- Waiting in line at the supermarket
- Shopping in a department store for perfume
- Being a spectator at a basketball game
- Taking your driving road test
- Visiting the gorilla cage in the zoo
- Being inside a haunted house
- Making a deposit at the bank
- Being at the mall at night
- Asking a teacher for missed work
- Teaching a young child to ride a bike
- Giving first aid
- Watching the most boring, terrible movie
- Explaining your unpaid bill as the electric company threatens to turn off the power
- Meeting a very angry dog
- Flying on an airplane
- Showing off your waterskiing skills
- Being taken out by friends for a special dinner
- Singing in an opera
- Playing a very competitive game of Monopoly™

Another Look

Discuss the activity, based on the following questions:

1. What happened with personal communication in each situation?
2. Did miscommunication cause a problem and, if so, why?
3. How might that miscommunication have been avoided?
4. How could the situation have worked out in a more positive way?

Play It This Way!

Many movies, TV shows, plays, short stories, or novels could easily have ended quite differently than they did. Here's a chance to change the endings to one of these stories. You may create a romantic, tragic, mysterious, funny, or political twist to an ending. Perhaps, look at some one-act plays, famous plays such as *Death of a Salesman*, or scenes from Shakespeare. The group might focus on one show or just a play's ending. In several smaller groups, each group might act out its own peculiar twist to the ending of that show or play.

A Trip Back to Your Past

This is a valuable exercise for focusing on sensory detail, personal feelings, and imagination and on building connections.

1. Have the group divide into pairs.

2. One member of each pair thinks back to a most favorite scene or least favorite scene from his or her past, and then describes the scene to the partner:

- What did it look like?
- Who was there?
- What happened?
- What were some of the sounds, colors, smells?
- What did people say or do?
- What were your feelings during this scene?
- Why is it one of your favorite or least favorite moments?

3. The other member of the pair describes a favorite or least favorite scene to the first person.

This Is My Life

Choose one person to narrate a day in his or her life. As this person narrates, others come up to act out—with dialogue and movement or in pantomime—whatever the narrator describes. These scenes may be funny, serious, scary, or adventurous.

Advanced Version

The narrator describes a personal problem or concern. The audience asks the narrator questions about his or her views of the problem. These questions may be probing, encouraging the narrator to clearly express the problem and to offer solutions.

The scene could be done again—only this time, alternative ways of handling the problem are acted out. The narrator selects alternatives to be enacted to see what happens.

Three Stooges Scene

Have three to five people create their own scene or reenact a television show or commercial. The narrator and actors must speak and act in the hysterical, energetic way that the Three Stooges would act.

Opera Scene

Have three to five people create their own scene or reenact a television show or commercial. The narrator and all actors sing their parts in operatic style.

The Intersection

In this activity, people take a variety of points of view as ethnic and different-aged characters. It's a chance to explore how background, age, and experience can influence what one sees at an intersection.

1. Choose participants:
   - Two car drivers (use chairs for cars)
   - An old man in a 1985 Dodge truck
   - A well-dressed woman in her thirties driving a new BMW
   - A black woman with a baby standing on the corner
   - A young Native American boy
   - An elderly Japanese man
   - A middle-aged policeman
2. The two cars collide at an intersection. Both drivers get out and start arguing. The arguing can be done at first in mime and/or with improvised dialogue. The other actors, except for the policeman, have witnessed the accident.

3. The policeman enters, and the two drivers explain what has happened.

4. Each of the witnesses explains what he or she saw. In giving testimony, each actor must consider his or her heritage, gender, age, and economic status, and speak with those characteristics in mind.

5. Afterward, evaluate what each person said. What is the truth? Why might these people differ so greatly in what they claim to have witnessed?

The actors might choose to play stereotyped roles, or to break those stereotypes. Then, a discussion might focus on why the character reacted in that manner.

Consider what would happen if:

- one of the cars was a 1980 battered VW bug.
- an elderly person had been driving.
- a teenage African American had been driving.

Senior Citizen Panels

The elderly or senior citizens, people over sixty years old, have had experiences and have views and opinions about life that are often quite different from those of young adults.

Choose four people to play senior citizens. You might assign each some background history: one may be or may have been rich, another a teen runaway, a doctor, a journalist, a mechanic, a clerk, and so on. Given their backgrounds, have each in turn respond to some of the following questions:

- What has your life been like?
- What is it like now?
- What is the highlight of your life?
- What is the biggest disappointment?
- Who were the greatest influences on your life, and why?
- How do you think children have changed since you were a child?
- What kinds of things did you do for fun?
- What national event do you remember, and what is your opinion of it?
- What was school like? Kids' behavior? How did you feel about the school shootings?
- What are your experiences with war?
- What changes in technology or society do you remember most? Why?
- What inventions have affected your life? How?
- How has political leadership changed over the years?
- What dreams and hopes did you have for the future?
- What is it like to be old?
- What are some of the advantages of being elderly? Disadvantages?
- What are your views on life and death? Are you afraid to die?

Another panel might involve two young adults and two elderly people responding to some of the questions listed above.

Or, a panel of four young people could respond to some of the questions; for example, what schools were and are like, or their feelings about war.

Tabloid Tale

1. Photocopy twenty or thirty short articles or features from some tabloids.
2. Cut out the headlines and put them in a box.
3. Each person picks a headline from the box.
4. Taking turns, each person uses the selected headline as the basis to create a story. Some wild stories happen!
5. After the person tells the story behind the headline, read the story that was actually in the tabloid.
6. Discuss what types of writing and psychology are used in tabloid stories, and for what effect.

What That Quote Really Means!

Maybe you've seen the movie or play or read the book, and maybe you haven't. It doesn't matter. Choose a quote from the ones below or from other sources. Then explain why it was said and what it means.

- "God was disappointed in Man, so he made the monkey."
- "Friends, Romans, Countrymen, lend me your ears!"
- "They shall beat their swords into ploughshares."
- "Win one for the Gipper!"
- "Good night, Mrs. Calabash, wherever you are!"
- "A woman, a dog, and a walnut tree."
- "They do taste kind of funny / But it keeps them on the knife."

Shakespearean Scene

Have three to five people create their own scene or reenact a television show or commercial. The narrator and actors must speak in Shakespearean language and phrasing.

The Scandalous Fruits and Vegetables Soap Opera

Here's a chance to create a new soap in which the characters are fruits and vegetables. Become a dramatic fruit or vegetable caught in the grind and puree of life! Create dramatic, life-threatening situations if your characters are celery stalks, stale cabbages, sweet peas, crab apples, thorny pineapples, rough rutabagas, subterranean potatoes, and so on.

The Vader View

Star Wars is told mainly from Luke Skywalker's, Princess Leia's, and the rebels' point of view. However, Darth Vader views the events and characters in the *Star Wars* trilogy from a very different point of view. After all, Darth represents the emperor and the official government. It's the rebels who are causing all the problems.

Ask the groups to imagine they are Darth Vader. How would they describe such characters as Luke Skywalker, Princess Leia, Han Solo, Chewbacca, R2-D2, C-3PO, Jabba the Hutt, the emperor Palpatine, and themselves? What they don't know about the character can be imagined using their observations of the character's actions, behavior, speech, and past. Have them give specific, concrete details. Remember, this takes place in space in a galaxy long ago. It's like a "back-to-the-future" in the future.

Fill in the form below. Each person imagines himself or herself as Darth Vader. How would Vader describe characters such as ...:

Character: _____

Appearance: _____

Family Background: _____
_____

Education: _____
_____

Work/Occupation: _____

Hobbies: _____

Bad habits: _____

Entertainment: _____

Politics: _____

Strongest characteristic: _____

Weakest characteristic: _____

Likes to eat: _____

Favorite movie: _____

Favorite gadget (not one shown in the movie trilogy): _____
_____

Now, either with excerpts of scenes from one of the *Star Wars* movie scripts, or simply by creating a scene you remember or by improvising, have the group act out the character roles from Darth's point of view.

The Really Old Commercial

ere's an opportunity to be an inventor, just like Benjamin Franklin and his swim fins!

1. Divide the group into small groups or pairs.
2. Have each group brainstorm some type of pre-1900 product, activity, or service they would create and advertise. They must not use any twentieth-century materials or technology.

   Brainstorming means to make a list of anything that comes to mind in a set period of time—perhaps fifteen minutes. Don't judge; write anything and everything down no matter how ridiculous it seems at the moment.

   A beginning brainstorming list might include:

sugar	ship	wood
clock	sailor	farmer
horse	cow	duck
barn	wool	clothes
log cabin	war	gun
bow	hunting	dancing
deer	tepee	mountain man

bear	politician	stagecoach
sails	Puritan	bridge
steeple	cowboy	saddle

3. At the end of fifteen minutes, have each group look at what they have written down. (They must choose two items and brainstorm these for ten minutes.) For example, for "ship" and "deer," the lists might look like this:

Ship: sailors, water, waves, salt, ocean, rope, sails, captain, mops, the mast, ladders, compass, shipwreck, rocks, sharks, gruff, rough, lonely, fish, whales, angry, hardworking, dangerous

Deer: grass, leaves, hide, hooves, race, doe, buck, antlers, fawn, gentle, beautiful, brown, thickets, Bambi, hunted, cars, family, forest, leaping, running

4. Each group considers what invention might come from this. For "ship" and "deer," for example, how about a deer cream that makes sailors gentle and better family men? Or a special compass that would give a ship the speed and leaping ability of a deer? With a little crossbreeding, they might invent the deer-shark!

5. For the product, service, or activity created, each group determines:
- its physical description
- its unique qualities
- its value to someone
- how it's made
- its benefits
- its uses
- what it improves

6. Each group creates a headline, logo, or motto for the invention that will catch their audience's attention. They should use one of the following traditional advertising techniques:

- A famous person testifying about the product or service
- The Happy Face having a great time using it
- Successful people who use it
- Everyone's using it!

7. Each group performs the commercial.

What's Inside Your Head?

ave people answer the following questions:

- What's a word or phrase you like the most, and why?
- What's a word or phrase you hate the most, and why?
- What's the nicest thing that ever happened to you?
- What's the worst thing that ever happened to you?
- What's the strangest thing that ever happened to you?
- If you could sit around a campfire with any person, living or dead, who would it be, and why?

- If you could star in any movie, what would it be?
- How could the world be a better place?
- How could you make this world a better place?

The Soap Opera of the Gods

How would the ancient gods behave if they lived in today's world? How might they be involved in situations concerning education, family, children, recreation, politics, entertainment, romance, war, poverty, work, or ecology?

Have the group choose some gods and goddesses to portray. They might mix gods from different cultures to create scenes with different points of view. To develop these a little further, they could research a few gods, create their characters, and bring into play their backgrounds. The following information is based on Arthur Cotterell's *A Dictionary of World Mythology* (New York: Oxford University Press, 1986).

1. Greek and Roman gods are immortal.

Zeus: god of the skies, chief god, hounded by Hera, his wife.

Venus: goddess of love, jealous, married to the crippled Vulcan.

Mars: god of war.

Ceres: goddess of grain and growing crops; her daughter, Persephone, is abducted by Hades (Pluto), the god of the dead.

Prometheus: a Titan who stole fire from the gods to give it to humans and is chained to a rock to have his liver devoured daily by a vulture.

2. Norse gods are mortal; live on Asgard, separated from Earth by the Rainbow Bridge; and know they will die on the Day of Doom.

Odin: chief god and one-eyed god of wisdom, royalty, and heroes.

Thor: the warrior god with his thunder-hammer, defender of common soldiers; he rode in a chariot pulled by goats.

Frey and Freya: brother and sister of the fields, grain, sun, and rain; they favor the farmers; Freya rides in a cart pulled by cats.

Loki: the trickster god, "father of lies," who saves the gods and then kills the god of beauty and brings on the destruction of the world.

3. Egyptian and Middle Eastern gods come from the land of desert, hot sun, the Sphinx, pyramids and hidden passages to the land of the dead, and the great Nile River.

Pharaoh: the all-powerful god-king of this world and the next.

Imhotep: architect of the Sakkarah pyramid and later the god of healing.

Inanna: Sumer goddess of love, fertility, and war.

Moloch: the fire god, who demands human sacrifices.

4. When we speak of Asia, we must remember that this term refers to many different peoples and countries: Japan, Mongolia, China, Korea, Malaysia, Thailand, parts of Turkey, India, and others. Each group of people has its own gods and myths.

Amaterasu: the Japanese sun goddess, drawn forth from a heavenly rock; her brother, Susanowo, is the mischief-making storm god.

Buga: chief god of the Tungus people in Siberia; he created the first people, iron hearts, fire-warmth, water-blood, earth-bones, and flesh.

Hari Hara: the Indian Buddhist god of growing and re-moving; he represents opposites.

Tsao Chun: in China, the kitchen god, the kind man-god who prepares good food for all to live long lives.

5. Africa, like Asia, is a huge continent that includes many peoples and countries, such as Ghana, Kenya, South Africa, Madagascar, Tunisia, and Ethiopia. Most African peoples believe there is one, all-powerful, all-knowing god who is everywhere.

Aigamuxa: dune-monsters with eyes in their feet who devour people.

En-kai: the sky and rain god of the Maasai people.

Jok: the creator god of the people of Zaire and Uganda, who believed their ancestors existed in the form of snakes or in rocks.

Your Trip to the Psychiatrist

1. Choose two participants: a psychiatrist and a patient. Put several chairs together to make a couch in the psychiatrist's office.

2. The patient enters and sits or lies on the couch. At the psychiatrist's suggestion, the patient then reveals a strange dream he or she has had. The patient might even rise and act out the dream.

3. The psychiatrist gives an interpretation of the dream and what it means for the patient. The psychiatrist might act the interpretation out.

Find a Character

There are characters all around us, some human, some not.

1. Each participant goes out and observes a character—a family member or a friend—a person at the mall, at a sports event, or some other public place.

2. Each person makes a list of how the chosen character looks, dresses, moves, speaks, and relates to others. Include details. Perhaps write down some of what that character says.

3. Then, using imagination, each participant determines:
   - What that character is thinking and feeling
   - Why the character is at this place
   - The character's history, family, work, and problems

4. Now, as a scene with dialogue or a monologue, each person shares character observations and conclusions with the group.

A few safety concerns: Participants should not follow the character, put themselves at risk, or be obnoxious. It is much better to observe and use one's imagination to create the character.

Cartoon Character Feast

Invite some famous cartoon characters (friends playing their favorite cartoon character) to a feast. The following are some possibilities:

- Daffy Duck
- Mickey Mouse
- Porky Pig
- Tweety Bird
- Wilma Flintstone
- Space Ghost
- Bashful the dwarf
- Popeye
- Felix the Cat
- Snow White
- Homer Simpson

What is the dinner conversation like? Remember to keep in character. The character conversation will develop better and more easily if the focus is on things that actually happened. Describe with detail, feeling, and dialogue as if each character were telling a story. Depending on their level of sophistication, children might just describe what happened at the cartoon character feast. Teens and older might act out the roles with dialogue, portraying the characters.

Disney-Type Scene

Have three to five people create their own scene or reenact a television show or commercial. The narrator and actors must speak in sweet, syrupy, Disney-style language and phrasing.

Charades

Playing charades is an excellent way to learn to think quickly and creatively while standing in front of an audience, under time limitations, focusing on connecting and communicating with the audience. The participants in this game can be individuals or teams.

Preparation

1. Pass out two or three slips of paper to each person.
2. On each slip, every person is to write down the name or title of one of the following:
   - book
   - famous person or character
   - movie
   - TV program
   - song

Each name or title must be no more than five words long.

3. Each person then writes the category or categories under which that name or title might fit. For example, *Dracula* would be a character as well as a movie and a book. So a person's first slip of paper might be:

> Name/Title: *Dracula*
>
> person/book

4. Each person writes a different name or title on another piece of paper, then folds the paper and keeps it a secret.

5. Collect the slips and put them in a pile. If the game involves teams, collect the slips for one team at a time. Place each team's slips in a pile separate from the other teams'.

6. In order for a team to guess the title acted out more quickly, they should decide, as a group, on certain standard gestures. For example, the gesture for a book might be cupped hands; for a TV show, rabbit ears; for a movie, the turning of a motion picture projector; for a song, pointing to one's mouth; for a person, pointing to one's self.

So, if the title is Ally McBeal, TV, person, the performer would start by demonstrating the rabbit ears and then pointing to himself or herself because the title of the show is a person's name.

7. The performer shows the number of words in the title by holding up a finger for each word, up to the five maximum words. For example, the song "The Cat Came Back" would be four fingers. The number of syllables in a word is usually shown by fingers placed on the forearm. For the word "raindrop," one would place two fingers on one's arm. Show short words—the, a, with—by holding the thumb and forefinger of one hand out parallel.

A word that rhymes with one in the title can be acted out if it appears that the group will guess it more quickly. Pulling on one's ear is the signal for "sounds like." When the group guesses the word being acted out, they must guess the rhyming word that will fit into the title. For example, if the word in the title is "here," it could be rhymed with "ear."

Making a chopping motion with one's hand indicates that the form of a word should be shortened; a stretching gesture shows the word form should be lengthened.

For the past tense of a verb, one waves a hand behind one's head; for the future tense, in front.

At no time may a performer mouth the words, draw letters or words in the air, or do counting to demonstrate a word in the title. For example, for "Henry VIII" the person is not allowed to count to eight on his or her fingers.

8. When someone guesses a word, syllable, or title correctly, the performer points to his or her nose or points to the guesser. Then the demonstrator goes on to the next part of the title.

Scoring

1. Establish either a two- or three-minute time limit for the class or team to guess the title. The timekeeper should not belong to the team.

2. The timekeeper records the time, in minutes and seconds, that it takes to guess the name or title correctly.

3. The person or team with the lowest cumulative time wins the game.

Playing the Game

1. One person or one person from a team is chosen to begin. If it's team play, the person chosen must pick from the other team's pile.

2. That person chooses one slip, reads the title silently, and spends fifteen to twenty seconds planning a strategy before the clock begins.

3. The moderator should silently read the slip chosen to see if the title is appropriate, within the word count, and possible to act out. For a first time, especially with shy people, the moderator may offer hints for how to think about and break down the title so that it can be acted out clearly for the others.

4. The person faces the audience or team and makes the sign for the category of the title.

5. The person shows the number of words in the title.

6. Using a finger count, the person shows which word he or she will act out first. (Choosing a major word in the title may allow the others to guess the title more quickly.)

7. The person either acts out the entire word or a portion of the title, or acts out a syllable of the word. For example, if the title is *Benji,* the person gets down on the floor and acts like a dog.

8. When someone guesses the word correctly, the perfomer next acts out another word in the title, first gesturing to indicate the position of that word in the title.

9. If the moderator sees that the audience doesn't understand the acting out and can't guess a word, he or she should encourage the performer to try something else to help the team members guess the word. Remember, time is passing.

For the first time or two, the moderator may want to enter after a round is finished and ask the group how that title might have been performed differently or more quickly. This helps people see alternative approaches, keep a more open and flexible mind, and learn why they may not have communicated as effectively as they had hoped.

Film Noir Detective Scene

Have three to five people create their own scene or reenact a television show or commercial. The narrator and actors must speak in 1930s tough, staccato, detective-style language and phrasing.

Character Masks

Masks can be very powerful. They give the person wearing the mask a chance to be free to act out how he/she feels the personality of the mask would feel and think.

1. Bring in—or have each member of the group bring in—character masks from Halloween or other times.
2. Place the masks in a large box.

3. Each person, without looking, chooses a mask and then acts out that character. Choose actions that portray that character's feelings.

4. Each person portrays that character with the opposite feelings and actions.

Alternate Versions

When the masks are chosen, two or three people act together in an improvised scene. Each person might take a few moments to discuss his/her mask's physical characteristics, emotions, and background.

The masks could also be an excellent way to stimulate family discussions: each member of the family chooses or draws a mask that acts out the way that person feels about a situation, or the opposite of the way that person feels.

Making Character Masks

Using papier-mâché, paper bags, or other materials, each person in the group makes a mask and then acts out that character individually or in group scenes.

Advanced Version

Each person makes one mask that represents how he or she appears to others, and a second mask that represents the inner person, or how he or she feels about himself or herself. The person then acts out these two "selves" in a scene, revealing the outward behavior and the inner feelings.

The Character Interview

Before going on stage to play a character part that has been prepared and rehearsed, there are some things to consider about that character—human or otherwise. Really good actors know their characters so well that they can tell you about that character's life offstage as well as on-stage. They know what their characters would eat for breakfast, how they would respond to a fire, whether they like to ice-skate, what books they've read, and so on. (This could be a worksheet to hand out.)

Character's name (make up one that fits): _____

Physical details: Height: _____   Weight: _____   Age: _____

Clothes: _____

Peculiar habits or features: _____
_____
_____

Voice and speech (sound, phrasing, pitch, word choice):
_____

Facial and body expressions with others (sarcastic,
depressed, joking, sincere, listening, etc.): _____
_____

History growing up: _____
_____
_____

Education/Work experience:_____
_____

Family life: _____
_____

Dreams/Wishes: _____
_____
_____

Dislikes/Avoids: _____
_____

Recreation: _____
_____

What would this character be like (use comparisons and specific details):

As an animal? _____

As music? _____
_____

As a plant or flower? _____
_____
_____

Or, instead of making up a character, fill out the above for a historical person.

Character Letters as Reader's Theatre

1. Choose a folktale. Then choose one person to represent each main character in that story.

2. Each person writes a letter telling what happened in the story from his or her character's point of view. The letter should capture the feelings, language, and views of that character.

3. Stage a reader's theatre with each person reading his or her character's letter. A narrator might begin the story, or summarize the story and introduce each character, who then reads the letter.

4. If there are too many students to participate in one folktale, then do several folktales. The group might try writing the letter in a mysterious language. The person who has written the letter keeps a description of what was actually written. This isn't revealed to the performers until they perform what they think the letter means. The letter writer or reader can clue the performers through voice inflection and emotion.

Personal Letters

Choose two actors to come on stage. One actor is downstage left; the other is mid-stage right. Each actor "writes" a letter to the other, including good descriptive detail in it.

The first actor reads his or her letter out loud; then the second actor answers that letter, adding his or her own personal news, insights, and feelings.

Here are some possible combinations:

- A father in prison writes to his son.
- A son in the Vietnam War writes to his mother.
- A sister writes to her brother on Mars.
- A father who deserted his daughter years ago writes to her.
- A college student writes to a friend who works in a fast-food restaurant.
- A patient writes to her psychiatrist.
- A person who has had a car accident writes to his insurance agent.
- A fan writes to a famous author.

Consider changing the people above, but using the same situation. For example, a mother may have deserted her daughter.

A Chance for Historical Drama

1. Brainstorm some scenes from American and/or world history. For example:

- Vikings in Canada
- the Pilgrims landing
- American Revolution
- gunfight at the OK Corral
- slavery
- cowboys
- Mississippi River showboat
- invention of the electric lightblub or telephone

- Columbus or Coronado
- Frontier Town
- Boston Tea Party
- assassination of Lincoln
- Civil War
- The Alamo
- Captain Kid the pirate
- home during World War I

2. Divide the main group into smaller groups of three to six people.

3. Assign each group to perform the same historical scene, but staged from a different point of view. For example, the first group might do the traditional historical account. The next group performs from the point of view of the common soldier or citizen. Another group acts from a woman's view of the event, or a black or Asian or Native American view. A group may present the victim's or loser's view.

4. Discuss what happened, the feelings expressed, and the results and effects of that historical moment.

Alternate Version

Have each group do a different historical scene. Each scene must be from a nontraditional historical view and include human characters and feelings. Focus on one minority's point of view—for example, women or Native Americans—and have each group act out a variety of American historical scenes from that group's point of view.

Historical Splits

1. Divide the group into pairs. Each pair creates and outlines or writes an original scene between two characters. The scene should be about three to five minutes long.

2. Each pair chooses one character from pre-1930 American history and a well-known personality from twentieth-century television, politics, books, movies, radio, or recent events. Here are some character possibilities:

Historical (pre-1930)	Modern (post-1960)
Abraham Lincoln	Martin Luther King
George Washington	Michael Jordan
General Custer	John Lennon
Sitting Bull	Barbara Walters
Pocahontas	Madonna
Andrew Carnegie	Elvis Presley
Calamity Jane	Marilyn Monroe
Buffalo Bill	Toni Morrison
Babe Ruth	Sammy Sosa
Benedict Arnold	Richard Nixon
Erik the Viking	Oprah Winfrey
Thomas Jefferson	Tiger Woods
Al Capone	Phil Knight (Nike)
Thomas Nast	Hillary Clinton
Harriet Beecher Stowe	Homer Simpson
Mark Twain	Robert Frost
Thomas Edison	Gloria Estefan
Shoeless Joe Jackson	Bill Gates
John Wilkes Booth	Lee Harvey Oswald
Jim Thorpe	Bill Cosby

3. These ingredients should be used:
- Description of the scene (time and place)
- Description of what happened just before this scene
- How characters move on stage in the scene, using terms like "downstage right" or "upstage center"
- The facial expressions, attitude, and physical gestures used by characters when saying their lines
- Emotions expressed or revealed by the characters when they speak

4. Facts about the famous person's life can be looked up in a history book or encyclopedia. The pair should decide what these two American figures—one historical and one modern—would discuss, or what situation might develop. For example, Bill Gates might meet Erik the Viking to discuss creating a computer game about Erik's voyage to this continent. Would they meet in Viking times or in modern times? How would the character who is out-of-place in time react to what he or she sees? What would be some problems and confusion in communication?

As another example, what would it be like if Michael Jordan challenged George Washington to a game of "Horse!"? More than likely, George would bring his horse. What would happen when Michael tried to explain the game to George?

5. The pair creates a serious or comic situation or conflict between the characters. It could be a melodramatic scene, a misunderstanding, a spy scene, or a social event. One character could interview the other.

6. The pair writes out the scene with dialogue, emotions, and character movement.

7. After writing and polishing the scene, the pair should memorize the dialogue.

8. The pair blocks the character movements on stage and rehearses for performance.

9. Stage the performance.

If I Were President ...

1. Imagine being elected president of the United States.

2. Have each person list the top three problems facing our country. They should describe each problem and both sides of the issue.

3. Then, with their power as president, each person decides how best to resolve the problem, and what the results will be for everyone involved.

4. The rest of the group reacts to the president's decisions and explains why they feel that way.

Laws I'd Like to See Passed

Imagine having the power to change any current laws, pass new laws, or repeal laws. What would you do? And why would you change that law?

1. The group might review how a bill is proposed and made into a law.
2. Introduce ideas for bills to the group.
3. Take a straw vote to determine the top five ideas that people would like to see become laws.
4. Set a time limit and debate the merits and effects of each of these five bills.
5. After the debates, take a vote on these bills to determine which will become law.

If I Could Change American History ...

I magine having the power to change any event in America's history. What would it be? Have the group decide what changes they would make, and why. With the changes you would make, what effects would these changes have on the future of America and American people?

If I Could Change World History ...

C onduct the same activity as above, only considering events in world history.

Changing Family Values

1. Using a blackboard or butcher paper, have the group brainstorm some family values for early Americans. For example:

- obedience to parents
- honesty
- telling stories
- possessions
- relationship between parents
- relationship between parents

- work
- helping neighbors
- eating together
- money
- education
- relationships between siblings

2. Now, make a list of contemporary American values, perhaps including some of the above-mentioned values.

3. Divide the group into groups of three to five people.

4. Have each group select one value to interpret and act out in a scene from early America and a scene in today's America.

5. Discuss the changes between then and now. Why have these values changed, and what have been the effects on individuals and on society?

Character Drama for "Family" Situations

1. Have the group choose a specific family problem, or a general one: peer pressure, drugs, parent restrictions, finding a job, dating, and so on.

2. Each person in the family or group assumes a character role in the scene. (It's probably best not to play himself or herself.) Let's say it's a scene about peer pressure to shoplift. Roles might include the bully, the person pressured, the friend of the person pressured, a member of the bully's group, an elderly person, the shop owner, a customer who sees the shoplifting, and a policeman.

3. Each character would then explain the following:
- Who he or she is
- What the situation is
- His or her feelings, emotions, or thoughts
- The meaning of this event to that character and to others
- The event's immediate and future results

Critical World Issues

1. Using a blackboard or butcher paper, brainstorm with the group a list of critical world issues. For example:

- guns
- the poor
- global warming
- gap between the
  rich and the poor
- school problems
- latchkey children
- cigarette smoking

- violence
- the homeless
- loss of the rain forest
- too much government
- too many taxes
- peer pressure
- drugs

2. Divide people into small groups and have each group choose an issue to act out in a scene. Give each group time to organize.

3. The group could act out the issue and then a possible solution. Or, a group might do the scene in pantomime and then with dialogue. A group could do the reverse: act out the scene first with dialogue, and then pantomime.

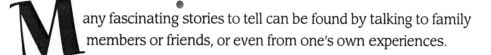

Family Tales

Many fascinating stories to tell can be found by talking to family members or friends, or even from one's own experiences.

1. Each person makes an appointment to interview family members or friends in person or by phone, recording the interview on tape. Holidays and family gatherings or visits are a great time to do this. It's amazing what one can learn by taking the time to ask questions and listening to people's responses!

2. In the interview, questions should be phrased so that the subjects cannot give yes/no or very brief responses. So, instead of asking, "When were you born?" ask, "What's the earliest memory you have as a child?" or "When you were born, what was life like—school, work, entertainment, and family life?" Questions for family or friends might be:
- How did your family come to America?
- What was it like during the war?
- How did Mom and Dad meet?
- Who was your family hero/heroine?
- Where and how were you born? How did your parents choose your name and what does it mean?
- What is the funniest thing that ever happened to you—or to someone else?
- What things did you do as a young child to make people laugh?

- What is the saddest thing that happened to you—or to others?
- What was a moment of terror or danger?
- What were some childhood accidents?
- What are some memories of schools: teachers, bullies, friends, happenings?
- Are there any family ghosts?
- What are some family sayings, and how did they come to be?
- Who is an odd family character?
- What was life like in another place or time?
- What was your first job? What happened at work?
- Describe celebrations, weddings, holidays, vacations.
- Describe some sad times: funerals, feuds, floods, earthquakes.
- What were some pet, farm, zoo, or wildlife experiences?
- What historical events made an impression on you?
- What was it like for you or someone you knew during the Great Depression, when JFK or Martin Luther King Jr. was assassinated, during the civil rights marches, when humans landed on the moon?

3. After the interview, each person learns the basic story and characters, then builds the story, adding physical descriptions and behaviors of the main characters, and creating dialogue. Details about the scenes—sounds, smells, sights, feelings—should be included.

4. Each person tells the characters' stories, making the listeners feel as if they were there.

Good Advisor/ Bad Advisor

1. Select three people: one is to be the person with a problem, another the good advisor, and the third the bad advisor.

2. The person stands in the center with an advisor on each side, and states some problem or conflict (or the group may suggest one). For example, a conflict may be:

- "Should I steal the money?"
- "Should I take the car without permission?"
- "Should I tell my parents about getting sent to the principal?"
- "I can sneak out and meet Carol (or Jim) after everyone's asleep."
- "I really hate him, and I'm going to tell him so!"
- "So what if they're using? They're my friends!"
- "Should I kill myself?"

3. The good advisor and bad advisor alternate with advice on how the person should act or behave. Each advisor states three to five reasons why the person should behave either in a good way or a bad way.

4. The person must then rationalize, out loud, what his or her choice will be, why, and what the consequences will be both short-term and long-term for everyone involved.

You Really Look Down!

1. Choose two people to come up front. In setting the problem, they pretend to be of any age and gender and in any location of their choice.
2. One person is very "down," or depressed, about a personal problem. He or she describes the problem to the other person.
3. The other person helps the first one deal with the problem through positive reinforcement, understanding feelings and point of view, encouragement, and/or creative problem solving.
4. After the scene, ask the group to discuss:
   - What they see as the real issue
   - The person's feelings and point of view
   - How encouragement was given and can be improved upon
   - Other ways to approach or deal with the problem

   Issues might include:
   - "I can never blow a bubble."
   - "My parents are getting a divorce."
   - "I just wrecked the car."

How Do I See Me?/ How Do I See You?

How do we see ourselves? And how do others see us? Let's find out.

1. Give everyone a paper and pencil.

2. Sitting separately and quietly, each person writes down what first comes to mind when thinking of himself or herself as:
- A body of water: colors, flow, temperature, setting
- An animal: type, movement, temperament, size, color, setting
- Music: tempo, type, dynamics, setting
- A child of three: personality, energy, behavior, friends, activities
- Your life in ten years or more
- An elderly person: personality, energy, the life lived, friends, activities

3. Everyone keeps his or her notes private for now. They must not revise whatever they wrote down. Usually the first image or impression is the most accurate.

4. Have the group form into pairs, choosing someone they don't know well or at all.

5. Facing the other person, and not talking, each person writes down how he or she imagines the other person in the five categories above.

6. When finished, the pairs silently exchange their sheets of images.

7. Each person compares his or her own images with those given by the other person.

8. If desired, the pairs may ask each other why they reacted that way. This discussion must be kept low-key and focus on understanding and acceptance—and the fact that the pair members don't know each other well. Depending on how people feel in the group, they might discuss what happened, how they felt about this experience, why they felt that way, and any questions they have.

I'll Be the Parent, You Be the Kid

1. Two to four people participate. If this is a family activity, the parents play the roles of the kids, and the kids play the parents. If it is another group, two people play the parent roles, and two others the kids' roles. One sibling may play the other, but without parody and sarcasm.

2. The groups choose an issue. At first it might be best to choose a minor one, such as:

- Doing the dishes
- Going to bed on time
- Taking care of the dog

- Watching too much television or certain types of programs
- Not getting a chance to do what you want to do

3. Each participant presents a different point of view.

4. The family or group tries to resolve the issue using a give-and-take approach. For example, one could say, "I might be able to help you with this problem if you could help me with the concern I have." Or "Can't Say No!" activity approach (see page 28).

5. With teenagers, more serious issues could be acted out: drugs, friends, dating, the future, the car, stealing, cheating, lying, lack of freedom, or trust.

If I Could Change My Personal History ...

Ask the group to imagine that they have the power to return to a moment or moments in their past and to change what happened to them or what they did at those moments.

- What would they change?
- How would they change it?
- What would be the effects of this change on their lives now and in the future? What would the effects be on their family's life in the future?

Alternate Versions

1. A person might reflect and write their answers as a journal-type entry and not share it.

2. In a family sharing activity, each family member might share one or two moments.

- What happened as a result of each moment?
- What would that person change and why?
- How would that change have affected what's happened to you as a member of the family?

  Other members of the family may be allowed to offer positive or constructive comments, or may just listen and accept the person's statement.

3. In a way similar to the family approach, a group of young people with similar backgrounds or ages may offer their personal views of what each would change in his or her life. Then the other members in the group may comment about what the person said, depending on what the person telling asks from the group.

Character Changing

1. Have each person choose a character-conflict scene from a folktale or a comic strip. Or, write character names and conflicts on pieces of paper, put them in a box, and have each person pull a name out.

2. Have people take the roles of the characters in the conflict and act out the scene, improvising dialogue, actions, body positions, and facial expressions that would help the conflict be resolved in more positive and productive ways. For example, a group might choose the scene in which:

   - Rumpelstiltskin asks for the baby he's been promised.
   - Hansel and Gretel deal with their stepmother.
   - Garfield does some sly tricks.
   - Lucy, Charlie Brown, and Snoopy get into a situation.
   - Hagar the Horrible gets in trouble with his wife.

Story Starters

1. Brainstorm some characters and settings with the group. Here are some possibilities:

Characters	Settings
A lizard	A jungle
An orphan girl	The moon
A spoiled rich lady	Prehistoric cave
An old hermit	Computer store
A mad inventor	Under a house
A tuskless walrus	A pirate ship
A businesswoman	A zoo
A house father	Under the ocean

2. Have the group make up different combinations of the characters and settings. How about a story about a tuskless walrus who lives on a pirate ship, or a mad inventor who opens a computer store, or an old hermit who finds a home in a cage in the zoo, or an orphan boy who lives in the jungle and becomes a house father?

3. Brainstorm a third possible category to go with the character and setting combinations. For example:

Character and Setting	Plot
An orphan boy in a prehistoric cave	Lost
	Jealousy
An ant on a pirate ship	Finding a friend
A walrus in a grocery store	Solving a mystery

House father on
the moon
A businesswoman
living under the ocean
An inventor at the zoo

Searching for a treasure
Meeting a monster in
the jungle

4. With these three categories, there's a wealth of story possibilities to tell or write.

The Tallest Tale

Who can tell the biggest, tallest tale around? When people tell big lies, a tall tale, a real humdinger, they should tell it like it's nothing but the truth, the actual facts. For example, it might be the time they really did dig a tunnel through the center of the earth all the way to China! Or the snowball the teller made that was bigger than the Golden Gate Bridge!

Have each person tell a tall tale in such a way that the audience really believes it. The group can vote on the most convincing and entertaining tale.

The Three-Object Tale

1. This activity can begin in two different ways. Put ten to fifteen objects in a sack. The person chosen reaches into the sack and pulls out three items. The person might show the group the objects, or hide them from sight. Or, put the objects on a table for the person to choose. The person comes to the front of the room and chooses three objects.

2. The person spends two minutes thinking of a story that will include these objects as important components of the tale.

3. The person tells the tale.

4. If the objects have been hidden from the audience's sight, then they could try to guess what three objects were used in the story.

5. The leader might point out or hand the person objects, openly or secretly, to weave into a tale, or even have pictures of the objects in the sack. For example, if the objects are a chair leg, a plate, and a tree, the tale could be about a man who was *soooo* hungry that he chomped down a plate, gnawed a chair leg, and tried to devour an entire tree!

Create the Story Behind the Song

1. Bring in several different songbook collections: folk songs, children's, popular, show tunes, and so on. Or, ask each person to copy the lyrics of two songs on separate pieces of paper and bring them in for this activity.

2. Collect the song lyric sheets from each person.

3. Have one person randomly choose a song lyric from the papers. Allow that person a few moments to silently read the song lyrics.

4. To begin, the person reads the song lyrics, seated or standing, out loud to the group.

5. Then the person tells the group about the real story behind these song lyrics. For example, why did that boy row the boat down the stream? Was he frightened? Running away? On a foolish adventure?

6. For the shy or reluctant participant, have him or her sit, read the lyrics out loud (or, have someone else read the lyrics out loud), and then interview the person to help him or her create a story. Be gentle and encouraging in the questioning.

Use the five *W*'s and *H* journalism approach:
- Who was the main character?
- Where did he or she live or come from?

- Why did the character act or feel this way?
- What was the situation?
- When did all this take place?
- How did it begin and continue?
- Who were the other characters or the antagonists in the story?

7. After the interview, have the group leader or someone else in the group summarize the story discovered through this interview. It's important to show the shy or reluctant person that he or she did, after all, create a story from the song lyrics.

Story Theatre

We all know many folktales. Let's improvise and act some out. The main characters are familiar, and more can be added. Dialogue can be made up to fit the action and events. Here are some tales to tell:

"The Pied Piper of Hamelin"
"Snow White and Rose Red"
"The Emperor's Nightingale"
"The Princess and the Pea"
"It Could Always Be Worse"
"Jack and the Beanstalk"

"The Adventures of Tom Thumb"
"Chicken Little"
"The Frog Prince"
"Why the Sea Is Salt"
"The Ugly Duckling"

"The Three Sillies"
"Sleeping Beauty"
"The Sorcerer's Apprentice"
"Wicked John and the Devil"
"Beauty and the Beast"
"Town Mouse, Country Mouse"
"The Little Match Girl"
"The Three Billy Goats Gruff"
"Anansi and the
    Moss-Covered Rock"
"The Emperor's New Clothes"
"Hansel and Gretel"
"Aladdin and the Magic Lamp"
"The Gingerbread Man"
"The Bremen Town Musicians"
"Cat and Mouse in Partnership"
"The Fisherman and His Wife"
"Prometheus"
"King Midas and the
    Golden Touch"
"Persephone, and the Seasons"

"The Snow Queen"
"Little Red Riding
    Hood
"The Tinderbox"
"Snow White and the"
    Seven Dwarfs"
"The Magic Kettle"
"Rapunzel"
"Goldilocks and the
    Three Bears"
"Lazy Jack"
"The Shoemaker and
    the Elves"
"Rumpelstiltskin"
"The Brave Little Tailor"
"The White Snake"
"The Stonecutter"
"Medusa"
"Cupid and Psyche"
"Arachne"
"Noah's Ark"

To learn a folktale, find a good anthology in the 398 section of the library. Joanna Cole's *Best-Loved Folktales of the World* (Garden City, N.J.: Anchor Press, 1982) or Jane Yolen's *Favorite Folktales from Around the World* (New York: Pantheon Books, 1986) are excellent collections.

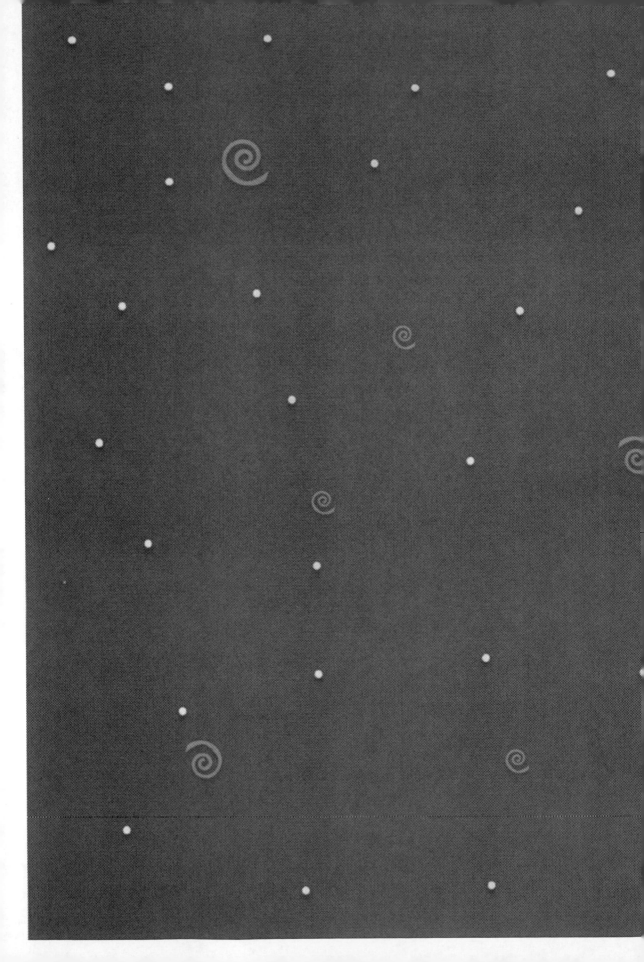

The Twin Arts of Storytelling and Performing

Some Tale-Thinking

ost folktales are more than just good stories. They say something about how to live life, about which characters are good models to follow or not good models, and how people should treat each other.

Many cultures from around the world share certain motifs in their stories. A motif is a subject or idea. For example, there are more than eight hundred Cinderella-type stories in the world, from the Vietnamese story to the Eskimo one of Tuna, as well as many versions in between. These tales may have the same motif of the evil stepmother and the good child wanting to escape, or the child who wants to receive recognition and love. The motif may be a brave girl rescuing someone, or the fool who accidentally solves the great mystery.

To better understand a story, consider the following:

- How does this tale show people's fears, hopes, dreams, or common problems?
- What is the life of the main character (the protagonist) like at the start of the story?
- In what ways does the main character change by the end of the story?
- What is the motif of the tale?
- How is the main character rewarded or not rewarded for the way he or she acts?
- How might someone apply what this story has to say about living to life today?

Types of Tales

Folktale: A tale from the oral tradition that has been passed on through generations as well as from place to place, with characters and scenes changing according to locations. These oral tales include myths, legends, fairy tales, fables, and tall tales. They usually portray people suddenly thrust into extraordinary times and situations.

Myth: Usually a tale that explains why something is the way it is: for example, why the sea is salty or why the sun is in the sky. Most myths involve gods or religion.

Fairy tales: A story that involves magic, usually through the powers of some magical figure such as an elf, fairy, gnome, witch, godmother, sorcerer, or genie.

Legend: A story told about a historical place, person, or event, with a kernel of fact or truth in it. The storyteller embellishes and exaggerates the fact or truth in the telling.

Tall tales: A wild, exaggerated tale about people or events told as if it were true. Many American tall tales—Paul Bunyan, Joe Magarac, John Henry—are stories manufactured by industry so that workers will work harder and produce more, becoming that industry's heroes.

Fable: A story that teaches a lesson or moral, focusing on the listener's ability to reason, understand, and learn the lesson or moral. With a fable, the listener doesn't become emotionally involved. Therefore, many fables use animal characters with which the listener cannot identify as representing him or her. ("I'm nothing like a wolf or a turtle.")

Literary tales: A story created and written by an author as if it were a folktale. Such authors include Hans Christian Andersen, Edgar Allan Poe, Mark Twain, and O. Henry.

Epic or Saga: Usually told in poetry form, it features a hero, such as Robin Hood, Beowulf, or King Arthur, who has a series of adventures.

Griot: An African who sings songs, tells stories, and recounts the history of his or her native land.

Learn a Tale to Tell

For more formal or traditional storytelling, people could learn to tell folktales or personal or family stories.

1. Have each person find a good anthology in the 398 section of the library. Joanna Cole's *Best-Loved Folktales of the World* and Jane Yolen's *Favorite Folktales from Around the World* are excellent collections.

2. Each person chooses a tale he or she likes and wants to share with others. The tale should be only two to four pages of text in length.

3. Each person reads the story through three times.
   - On the first read, focus on the action of the story and the order of the action.
   - On the second read, pay attention to each of the main characters: what each looks like and how each speaks and acts.
   - On the third read, concentrate on the scene detail: what each place or scene in the story looks like, feels like (colors, smells, sounds).

4. Each person then closes the book and tells the story out loud to himself or herself or to a friend. No matter how much the person forgets, it's important to finish the story.

5. The person rereads the story to find out any details he or she may have left out.

6. The person tells the tale again. It's okay to add or change parts of a tale. That's what happens with retellings: the story stays alive and changes all the time.

7. The source of the story should also be mentioned.

A Story to Learn: "The Sun, the Moon, and the Water"

Let's tell the Nigerian story, "The Sun, the Moon, and the Water."

Once, at the beginning of the world, the Sun and the Moon and the Water lived on the earth, and they were very good friends. Why, each day the Sun and the Moon would come to visit the Water. Water would swirl and wave and dance for its two friends. They all had a good time together.

One day, however, the Sun said, "We come every day to visit you, Water, but why don't you ever come to visit us at our home?"

Water gurgled and dripped. "It's simply because you have no place for me and all of my family: the oceans, the rivers, the lakes, the ponds, and the rain falling from the sky."

"We can solve that," said the Moon. "We'll dig a huge, huge hole and then all of you can come to visit."

So that's what the Sun and the Moon did. They dug a huge, huge, huge hole. When they had finished digging, they invited

Water to come for a visit. And Water came, rushing and flowing and gurgling, with all of its family: the oceans, the rivers, the lakes, the ponds, and the rain falling from the sky.

Water and its family stopped at the edge of the hole and asked politely, "May we enter?"

The Sun said, "Why, yes. Come ahead. That's why we dug this huge hole, just for your visit."

And Water did just that. It poured and poured and poured into that hole until the hole was half-filled. Then it stopped.

"Would you still like us to enter?"

The Sun looked at the Moon, and they both nodded "yes."

So Water poured and poured and poured into that hole until the hole was completely filled, right up to the top!

And again Water asked, "Do you still want us to enter?"

The Sun said, "Well, why not? There can't be that much more of you."

And again Water poured and poured and poured onto the land—until the Sun and the Moon were forced to climb to the roof of their house. The Sun and the Moon sat there looking down at Water.

"Shall we still enter?" asked Water one last time.

Well, by this time, the Sun was very angry and was feeling very foolish and said, "Certainly you can come in. There can't be much more of you now, can there?"

And so Water and all of its family poured and poured and poured and poured onto the land, swallowing up the house of the Sun and the Moon.

The Sun and the Moon were forced to climb all the way up into the sky. That's where they are today, and that's how they got there.

This story can be learned in a series of steps with a quick review of the order of events. It's important to remember that the story is to be learned, not memorized word for word.

1. The Sun, the Moon, and the Water lived on the earth and were friends.

2. The Sun and the Moon came to visit Water, but Water never came to visit the Sun and the Moon.

3. The Sun and the Moon decided to dig a huge hole so that Water could visit.

4. Water came and asked to enter, and filled the hole halfway.

5. Water filled the hole all the way.

6. Water kept pouring, and the Sun and the Moon had to climb to the roof of their house.

7. The Sun, feeling angry and foolish, told the Water it could still enter.

8. The Sun and the Moon were forced to climb into the sky— where they are today.

That's the story! With eyes closed, one could tell it out loud to oneself, or with eyes open, tell it to someone else. It should be told all the way through, no matter how much may have been left out. Then the story can be read again, this time focusing on what was skipped over. Tell it again!

Telling a Mind Picture

When you tell a story, tell your "mind picture," not just words. You, as the teller, see the story happening in your mind and invite the audience to see the story, too.

Each scene in a story is like a frame from a strip of movie film. As the movie frame passes through your mind, you, as the narrator, describe the scene to your listeners and assume the role of each speaking character. You should be so convincing, so involved in the scene and the movement of the story, that your listeners can almost see the story happening right before them. They can watch you pick the apple from the tree, lift the heavy stone, shiver with fright at the sight of the evil witch.

To tell mind pictures, don't memorize the story word by word; instead learn the story. This technique has been proven effective in the classroom. Students may learn the stories from notes they've taken or from books, but they can never have these notes or the books to use when they tell before the class or an audience. If the students did tell with notes or a book, they would have a crutch and might feel that they could not tell without notes.

When the storyteller learns the story, instead of memorizing it, he or she preserves the truly creative, living art of storytelling. I have, for example, told "The Spoon's Child" or "The Golden Arm" a hundred or more times. Each time the story changes. The story's never quite the same. I purposefully, or accidentally, include some new detail, a new twist, a different bit of description.

To avoid memorizing word for word, I play games with the story, testing myself while learning the story. Can I list the events or actions of the story in order? Can I describe the main characters' appearances and backgrounds? Can I start the story from some point in the middle and continue it? What about telling it from the end to the beginning?

The more fun you have learning the story, the more flexible and comfortable you feel with it, and the more alive and fresh the story will be when you tell it. The height of the storyteller's art is to be able to tell the story and flow with the unexpected changes. You are so involved with the story that nothing fazes you. To do this you must be aware that two stories are really being told at the same time: one inside your head and one to the audience.

If the teller hears that a new ingredient has popped into the telling, or realizes that an important detail has been left out, then the teller must be flexible and comfortable enough to decide immediately what to do. Is that new ingredient or the part that was left out so important that it changes the story? If it does, the teller must be able to adapt the new moment or include the missing part so smoothly that the audience doesn't notice the change or added detail.

Some stories contain a short rhyme, a magic spell, or an important phrase or dialogue that must be memorized. These are special ingredients, but for the most part, the rest of the story is alive.

Telling mind pictures frees the imagination to soar with the story and include the listeners as special passengers on the journey.

Performance Tips

1. Resist the urge to unconsciously unbutton or unzip or otherwise fiddle with your clothes while performing: it's distracting to the audience.

2. Set your feet, one slightly in front of the other, to avoid shifting from foot to foot unconsciously, moving your feet back and forth, or rocking your body.

3. Keep your body at a 45-degree angle, so that the entire audience can see most of you all the time. When you play two characters in a dialogue scene, face one character in a 45-degree angle one way, and then face the other way at a 45-degree angle when playing the second character. This also avoids the annoying phrases "he said" and "she said" whenever a character speaks in the scene. We know by position which character is speaking in that scene.

4. Pan so that you have eye contact with all your audience. Remember to have eye contact with those near you as well as those in the back. For those who feel uncomfortable looking at the audience directly, pick a spot above the audience's heads and pan using this spot. Don't look down at the floor. The floor stops your voice and the floor is not listening to you.

5. If the conclusion of your story doesn't feel right to you, change the ending so that it does. It's your story to tell!

6. Whatever your character is doing and feeling at a particular moment in your story, your face, body, hand gestures, dialogue, vocal tone and pitch, and word choice should all focus on bringing that moment to life for your listeners. Show the audience; don't have the characters report to them.

7. Do not wear a hat or allow your hair to cover or shadow your face so that the audience can't see your facial expressions clearly. Do not wear sleeves that hang over your hands or flap; such sleeves hide your hand gestures and the flapping distracts listeners from what you're saying. Don't wear hanging, clanging, or swinging jewelry that distracts the audience, or that tempts you to play with it while you're performing.

8. Avoid laughing or giggling at what you're doing: it makes your listeners feel you're not sincere and that you don't believe in the story you're sharing.

9. If characters or objects in your story are different sizes or at different heights, look up when you're lower and down when you're higher.

10. Keep your hands at your sides or in front of you when not gesturing. Keep your hands out of your pockets. Don't lock your fingers together in front of you or play with your fingers.

11. Be careful not to swallow or mumble the ends of sentences, or rush through your narrative part. Try to keep your voice toward the top of your throat. Think of arching your speaking voice up to the cavity near the top of your head.

12. Take a moment before you begin telling to your audience: inhale and exhale a few deep breaths to relax and open your throat.

13. Wait to begin speaking until you're on the stage in front of the audience. Don't begin talking as you're walking on

stage unless you've designed your performance that way for a special reason.

14. Keep the words you use appropriate to the time and culture of the story you're telling. For example, "Give me a break!" and "Hang in there!" are not suitable dialogue when telling "Ali Baba and the Forty Thieves."

15. If your story comes from a different culture—with some unusual words or character names or interesting concepts your listeners should know about—take time to introduce these or explain before you begin to tell your tale. In this way, your listeners will be prepared, can enjoy your story, and won't have to wonder what something means.

16. Begin your story with high but controlled energy. Step into the telling! This doesn't mean you should speed up your telling, but rather be completely focused on the story and connected with the audience. You can feel it when you're at this level.

17. Nervous? Every performer who goes before an audience should be nervous. A performer needs this nervous energy to gear up to "step into" the presentation. A confident, seasoned performer, one who knows the tales and how he or she wants to perform, controls this nervousness to focus the energy and improve the performance. An inexperienced performer may be so controlled by nervousness that he or she doesn't perform well.

18. Many stories have repeating phrases, ideas, and situations. For these it is usually more effective to repeat them in a different way by changing the emphasis, your tone and emotion, pacing, or phrasing. This is especially so in the "add-on" stories—for example, in which the dog asks the cat who asks the water who asks the skunk ...

19. A story is normally told in the past tense: the action has already happened. So the narrator should say, "John said," not "John says."

20. If you're portraying an animal or creature, then try to become that animal as much as possible. If you are a turtle, then move your head, neck, legs, and arms like a turtle would move.

21. Keep visible at all times. Don't get down on the floor to act out a role if your audience will not be able to see you.

22. Don't keep repeating "You know" over and over. Your audience didn't come to listen to what they already "know."

23. Don't wave your hands around. Keep your arms and hands at your sides until you clearly need them to make a gesture that brings your character to life at that moment. Gestures should support your story, not distract from it.

24. A story should be entertaining. You and your audience should enjoy sharing a tale well told. It's a group experience, and you are part of the group.

Telling Tips

As a storyteller, you continually learn, grow, and change along with your tales. The following is a list of skills to improve storytellings:

- **Vocal projection:** Can you be heard by everyone?
- **Clarity:** Is your speech clear and understandable?
- **Pacing:** Do you speak at a pace that's easy for the listeners to follow, but not so slowly that the story drags?
- **Characters:** Do you show the character through action and give some description of the character?
- **Dialogue:** Do you bring the characters to life by having them speak?
- **Words to avoid:** Do you avoid slang terms, "ums," "aahs," repeated "ands" that string sentences together, "you knows," and "he went" rather than "he said"?
- **Preparation:** Do you know your story so well that there's no chance of forgetting it?
- **Dramatic gestures:** Do you use your hands, eyes, face, and body to bring the characters and actions to life?
- **Intensity:** When you tell, do you hold your audience's interest? Does it feel as if there were a wall around you and your audience, and that you've moved into another world, another dimension?

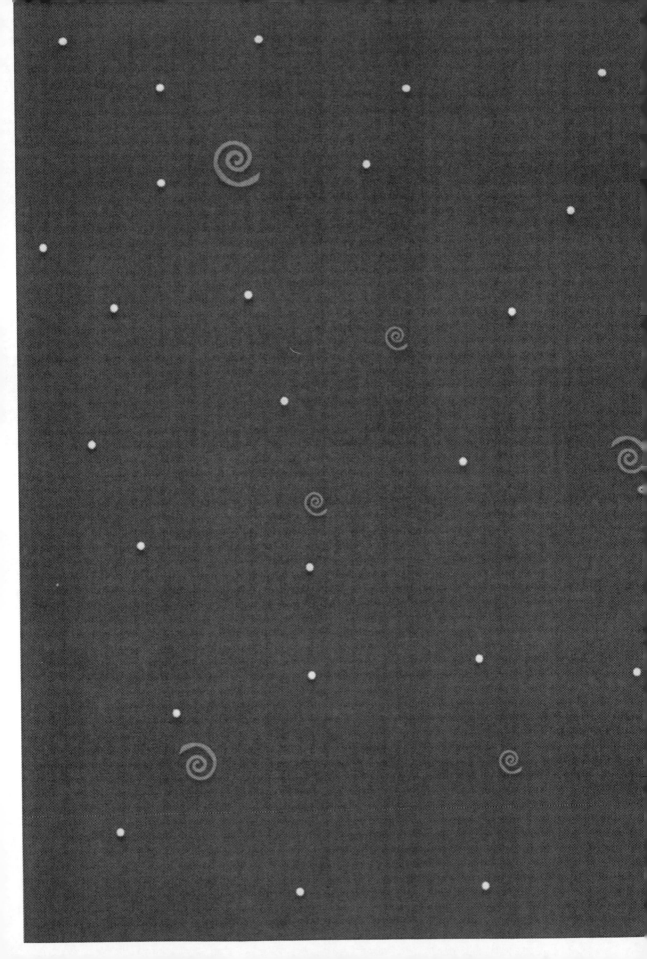

Appendix
of
Linked
Activities

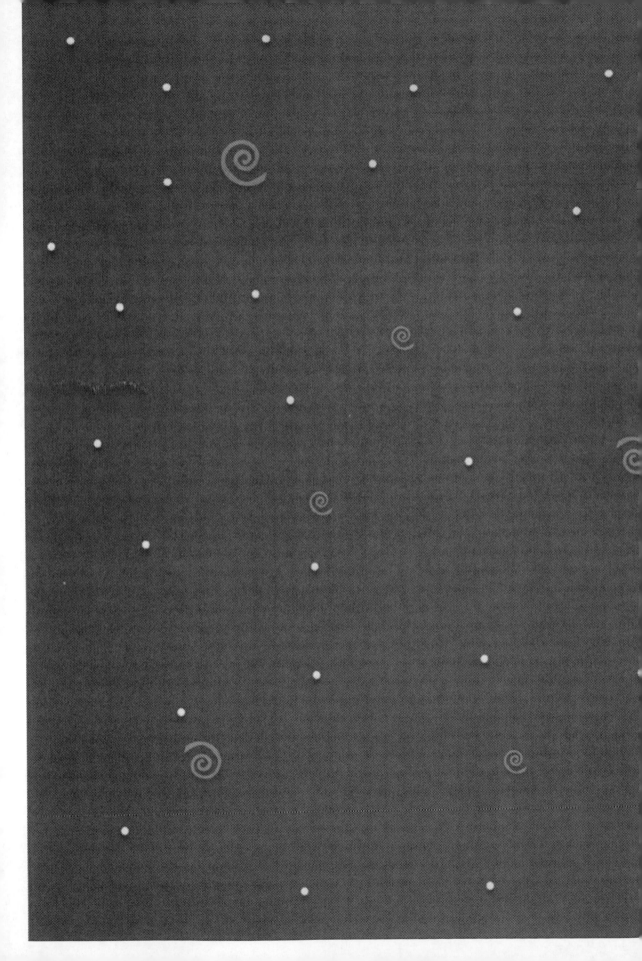

Group Activities

Skill-Building and Class Activities

The following activities and theatre games encourage creative thinking and skill-building, and offer a variety of ways to engage students of varying abilities in the curriculum. Many of these performance activities focus on developing speaking skills such as vocal projection, poise, clarity, word usage, gestures, panning and eye contact, organization, characterization, dialogue, and listening in nonthreatening and fun ways. These activities, of course, will need some modification or adaptation to your specific student and class needs and goals.

In terms of curriculum, many of these theatre games require that the student interpret and add human elements and multicultural aspects to history, or encourage the student to appreciate different points of view, solve problems, or perform or write in different genres. A number of these activities also encourage creative and interpretive writing.

Family and Counseling Activities

S tudies point out that the vast majority of parents find it very difficult to communicate with their children, especially teens. Children have similar difficulties communicating with their parents or other adults.

The following activities are meant to promote informal, nonthreatening ways in which both adults and children can freely express and share ideas and feelings. In turn, this can lead to greater mutual understanding and problem solving. Not only might these activities be useful in counseling situations, but they can also serve as icebreakers and work well for peer counseling groups Some of these activities may focus on sensitive issues not suitable or comfortable to share in a large group.

Curtains Up!

Storytelling Activities

Stories and storytelling have entertained and been enjoyed by people since they first communicated with cave drawings. Everybody has tales to tell. Anybody can be a storyteller just by sharing these tales, even personal ones, with others. Learning to tell tales well is a matter of focusing on some skills and improving through telling often and to different audiences.

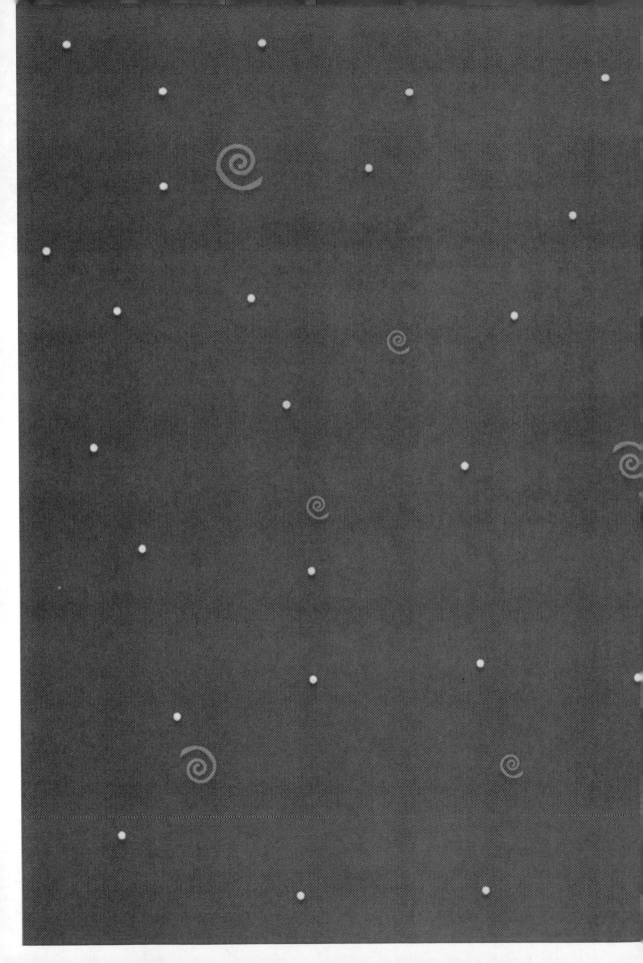

About the Author

S ince 1969, Robert Rubinstein has taught in the unique elective program at Roosevelt Middle School in Eugene, Oregon, where he created thirty-four curriculum classes, ranging from courses in monsters, King Arthur, and playwriting to folktales, storytelling, and teaching history through movies. Among these classes was the nationally known Troupe of Tellers, sixth- through ninth-grade students who performed for some three thousand students annually for twenty-four years. In 1983 the Troupe of Tellers received one of the state of Oregon's "Great Kids" Public Service Awards, and in the summer of 1993 the National Storytelling Conference invited the troupe to give an hour-and-a-half performance-workshop for storytellers and educators from around the world.

Robert Rubinstein wrote the internationally acclaimed book *Hints for Teaching Success in Middle School*, based on his teaching at Roosevelt. His fourth recording and first CD, *Strange Tales from Biblical Times*, appeared in 1999. His stories have been published in *The Ghost & I* and *Chosen Tales: Stories by Jewish Storytellers*. In 1990 he founded the Multi-Cultural Storytelling Festival, which annually brings in nationally known storytellers representing different ethnic and minority groups to perform for more than eight thousand students in schools and in the greater Eugene–area community.

Mr. Rubinstein lives in Eugene, Oregon, with his wife, three children (including Shoshanna, who performed for two terms in the Troupe of Tellers), Kira the dog, and Jaffa and Simcha the cats.

About the Illustrator

Libby Head, a junior at South Eugene High School when she created the illustrations for this book, has already achieved local artistic recognition. She has exhibited in her own gallery show, designed an art calendar, creates artwork on T-shirts, and won in-school art awards. She works at 19th Avenue Promotions in the graphic design and theatre department. While writing and illustrating her own children's books, Libby experiments with graphic design, drawing, and painting. She plans to become a teacher in elementary school.

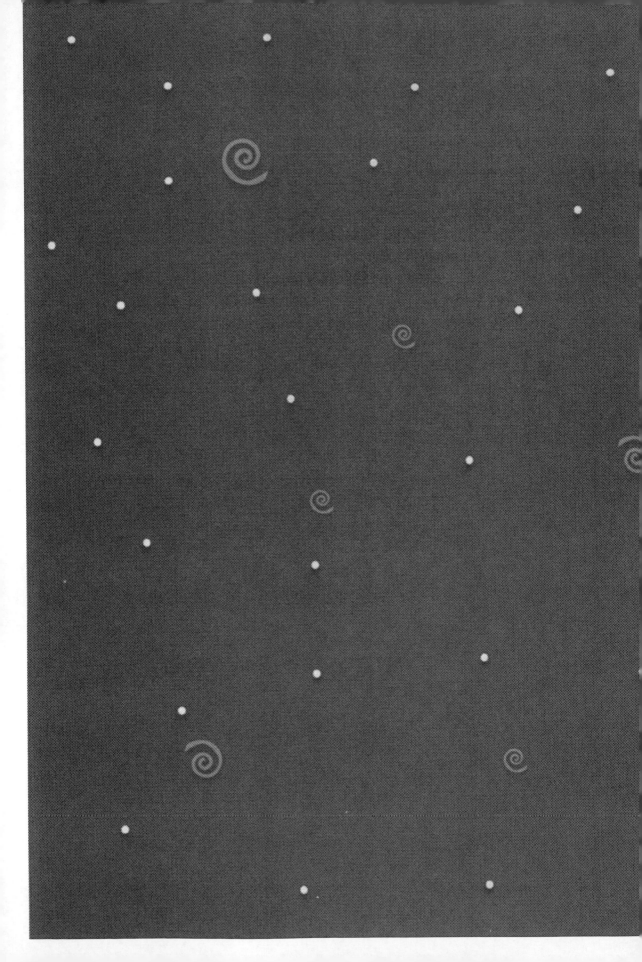

Bibliography

Anderson, Hans Christian. *Eighty Fairy Tales*. New York: Pantheon, 1976.

Baltuck, Naomi. *Apples from Heaven: Multicultural Folktales about Stories and Storytellers*. New Haven, Conn.: Linnet Books, 1995.

Booss, Claire, ed. *Scandinavian Folk & Fairy Tales*. New York: Avenel Books, 1984.

Botkin, B. A., ed. *A Treasury of American Folklore*. New York: Crown, 1944.

———. *A Treasury of Southern Folklore*. New York: Bonanza Books, 1949.

Chase, Richard. *The Jack Tales*. New York: Houghton Mifflin, 1943.

Cole, Joanna, ed. *Best-Loved Folktales of the World*. Garden City, N.J.: Anchor Press, 1982.

Courlander, Harold. *Cow Tail Switch and Other Ethiopian Stories*. New York: Holt, 1947.

Grimm, Jacob, and Wilhelm Grimm. *Complete Grimm's Fairy Tales*. New York: Pantheon, 1944.

Hamilton, Virginia. *The People Could Fly: American Black Folktales*. New York: Alfred A. Knopf, 1985.

Hume, Lotta Carswell. *Favorite Children's Stories from China and Tibet*. Rutland, Vt.: Charles E. Tuttle, 1962.

In-sob, Zong. *Folk Tales from Korea*. Elizabeth, N.J.: Hollym International, 1982.

Kelsey, Alice Greer. *Once the Hodja: Tales from Turkey*. New York: David McKay, 1967.

Kimmel, Eric. *The Adventures of Hershel of Ostropol*. New York: Holiday House, 1995.

———. *Be Not Far from Me: Legends from the Bible*. New York: Simon & Schuster Books for Young Readers, 1998.

Lester, Julius. *The Knee-High Man and Other Tales*. New York: Dial, 1972.

MacDonald, Margaret Read. *The Storyteller's Sourcebook.* New York: Gale, 1982.

———. *Twenty Tellable Tales.* Chicago, Ill.: Wilson, 1986.

Maguire, Jack. *Creative Storytelling: Choosing, Inventing, and Sharing Tales for Children.* New York: McGraw-Hill, 1985.

National Storytelling Press. *Best-Loved Stories Told at the National Storytelling Festival.* Little Rock, Ark.: August House, 1991.

Pavlat, Leo. *Jewish Folk Tales.* New York: Greenwich House, 1986.

Roberts, Moss, ed. *Chinese Fairy Tales and Fantasies.* New York: Pantheon Books, 1979.

Schram, Peninnah. *Jewish Stories One Generation Tells Another.* Northvale, N.J.: Jason Aronson, 1987.

Schwartz, Alvin. *Scary Stories to Tell in the Dark.* New York: Lippincott, 1981.

Schwartz, Howard. *Elijah's Violin and Other Jewish Fairy Tales.* New York: Harper & Rose, 1983.

Silo. *Tales for Heart and Mind: The Guided Experiences: A Storybook for Grownups.* San Diego, Calif.: Latitude Press, 1993.

Singer, Isaac Bashevis. *Zlateh the Goat.* New York: Harper, 1966.

Smith, Jimmy Neil, ed. *Homespun: Tales from America's Favorite Storytellers.* New York: Crown Publishers, 1988.

Spagnoli, Cathy. *Asian Tales and Tellers.* Little Rock, Ark.: August House, 1998.

Wolkstein, Diane. *The Magic Orange Tree and Other Haitian Folktales.* New York: Alfred A. Knopf, 1978.

Yolen, Jane, ed. *Favorite Folktales from Around the World.* New York: Pantheon Books, 1986.

Index

151

CPSIA information can be obtained at www.ICGtesting.com
Printed in the USA
240171LV00003B/9/A